The Book Lover's Guide to Chicagoland

D0107927

by
Lane Phalen

Brigadoon Bay Books
Hoffman Estates, Illinois

The publisher and author of this book assume no legal responsibility for the completeness or accuracy of the contents of this book nor any legal responsibility for any increase or decrease in the value of any enterprises, whether for profit or non-profit, by reason of their inclusion or exclusion from this work. Contents are based on information believed to be accurate at the time of publication.

Neither Brigadoon Bay Books nor the author have accepted payment from any firms or organizations for inclusion in this book.

Publisher's Cataloging in Publication
(Prepared by Quality Books Inc.)

Phalen, Lane.
   The book lover's guide to Chicagoland / by Lane Phalen.
   p. cm.
   Includes index.
   ISBN 1-88033-906-4

   1. Booksellers and bookselling--Chicago (Ill.)--directories. I.
Title.

Z475   381.45002
                                         QBI91-1340

Library of Congress Catalog Card Number: 91-74136

9 8 7 6 5 4 3 2 1

Printed by Walsworth Publishing Company of Marceline, Missouri

To my dear husband,
Rob,
who pushed me every step of the way.

Preface

On family shopping trips to the big city, my Mom, Dad, two sisters, and I would head for the malls. As they went into clothing stores, I would duck into a bookstore telling them to stop by and pick me up when they were done. Unfortunately, they always finished before I had and one of them would show up to drag me out of the store as I begged for just a few more minutes. Then I got smart--I used to crouch behind the shelves in the back of the store so that they couldn't see me from outside and would have to come into the store to get me. It didn't buy me a lot of extra time but even a few extra minutes in a bookstore used to make me happy.

There comes a time in all dating relationships when you recognize that you've found your soul-mate. That precious moment came for me when Rob and I stopped at a bookstore and he wasn't finished browsing until way after I was ready to go. I stood at the magazine section and watched him pluck a book from the shelf, read the back cover, flip through the pages and read a sample paragraph. I was his forever. That old sappy love face formed itself on my face: the dreamy eyes, the soft sighs, the tilt of my head as I watched him. No doubt about it, I was in love. The check-out girl asked if I was OK or if I needed to sit down. I regained my composure while he was paying for his three paperbacks, two hardbacks, and a magazine. He knew I was the woman for him when he saw that I had overflowing bookcases in all my apartment rooms.

He proposed marriage outside of a bookstore and we went in to celebrate. No, we didn't hold the ceremony in a bookstore but it was a temptation. All our books joined and lived happily ever after.

Whenever we travel, we make sure to check out the bookstores. You never know where you will find a treasure chest--Indianapolis and Seattle were the homes of our favorite surprises. Originally, this book was conceived as a joke. We were driving from Vancouver to Seattle and were going to have a couple of hours before our airplane took off. Naturally, we thought of Tower's Bookstore that we had visited two years earlier. On a dare Rob drove directly to the store with no wrong turns. It was at that moment that we knew we were addicted to books. It was a spiritual awakening.

Thus, the birth of this book. We thought we knew every good bookstore in the Chicago area but kept coming across treasures of which we were unaware. After our research, we knew of 400 bookstores in Chicago and it's suburbs. The research was a joy. We were obsessed and traveled from bookstore to bookstore. In some bookstores we just stood and experienced the atmosphere. In most, we fed our habit and bought books.

I have multiple sclerosis and have used a wheelchair for the past two years. In my pre-chair days, I thought the whole world was wheelchair accessible. As my husband and I visited stores, we were surprised to find that I was mistaken. Wheelchair accessibility plays a prominent part of this book. I purposely included this type of information. Most of the time, a wheelchair means a person can't walk, not that he or she can't read and enjoy the search. The same is true for the blind who are able to enjoy the growing number of books on tape so I've included information about book resources available for the blind. Please let me know if there are any ways I can improve the usefulness of this book for the disabled. To communicate with me, send a letter to Lane Phalen, c/o Brigadoon Bay Books, P.O. Box 957724, Hoffman Estates, IL 60195.

There are so many fascinating book-related activities in Chicago that I wanted to let the reader know about. Included are calligraphy, illuminated manuscripts, cartography, libraries, book collecting, and museums. I hope you will find these to be of interest to you. Check the bookstores out. You'll be as thrilled as we were to find these special little hideaways.

I plan to update this book periodically. If you know of any additional book related establishments in the Chicago area, please send me a note through the publisher or use the form at the back of the book.

I hope that this book will serve you well as a reference book. Next time you're looking for something different to do, check out one of these establishments.

Lane Phalen

Table of Contents

CHICAGO CENTRAL

Abraham Lincoln Book Shop

Civil War

357 W. Chicago Ave.
Chicago, IL 60610
312-944-3085
Hours: Mon.-Sat. 9-5

"We're a bit of an archeological dig," said Daniel Weinberg, proprietor of the Abraham Lincoln Book Shop. When you step into the store, you step into history. The wonderful thing is that you can take a piece of history home with you. In addition to books relating to the Civil War, you'll find documents, photographs, autographs, bronze and plaster busts, and limited edition military prints.

The 8,500 books in stock cover topics such as history, biography, and militaria presenting all of the United States past. Although the Civil War is their specialty, they also offer books about American history, the Napoleonic era, and the U.S. Presidency. Books are antiquarian, new, used, and reprints. They will take special orders.

As an added feature, the Abraham Lincoln Book Shop has their own "resident" artist who creates an original Civil War scene painting. Dan oversees special reproductions in limited signed editions.

Another unique offering is the sale of famous people's autographs. Dan explained that an Abraham Lincoln signature ripped from a document will sell for a few thousand dollars. A copy of the actual Emancipation Proclamation with the signatures recently sold for $275,000. In addition to Lincoln, autographs that Dan has for sale are Robert E. Lee, U.S. Grant, Andrew Jackson, George Washington and other Presidents.

Dan noted that the recent PBS series on the Civil War has "spilled gasoline on a fire already going out of control."

If you show up at the store on a Friday night, you may get a glimpse of the Civil War Round Table. The group, established fifty years ago, meets semi-monthly to discuss various aspects of the Civil War. It is the oldest world-wide Civil War organization of it's kind. Over 300 members come from various backgrounds and range from experts to newcomers. The discussions are not to be missed if you're a Civil War buff: speakers have included authors Bruce Catton and James McPherson. Their activities include touring battlefields. Some members do battle re-enactments for special functions.

"There are four chapters in Chicago," Dan explained. He proudly added that of all the chapters across the United States, this is the only one that is titled "The" Civil War Round Table with no qualifying identifier such as Chicago, Illinois Branch, etc.

A true Civil War enthusiast and historian, Dan also speaks to "sister" groups across the country and assists writers with specific research projects. Dan travels to such famous places as Gettysburg to attend shows and purchase relics and books for his shop.

The sad news for those in wheelchairs is that there are five steps to enter the store. Once inside, the store is completely accessible. A catalogue is available. Seating is available for patrons to sit and browse. Mass transit and parking are nearby.

Archicenter Bookstore

Architecture   330 S. Dearborn
                                  Chicago, IL 60604
                                  312-922-3431
                                  Hours: Mon.-Fri. 9-6; Sat. 9-5

The official bookstore of the Chicago Architecture Foundation, Archicenter carries over 2,000 books focusing on architecture. They stock over 100 books about Frank Lloyd Wright. Also available are gifts, coffee mugs, jewelry, and even gargoyles.

The Archicenter arranges over sixty tours of Chicago's unique architecture. Tours are conducted on foot, by bicycle, on buses, and even on boats. The bookstore is wheelchair accessible. Discuss tour options with the staff.

In January, 1992, Archicenter Bookstore will move to the Sante Fe Building at Michigan and Jackson.

Art Institute of Chicago-Museum Store

Art   S. Michigan & E. Adams
                                  Chicago, IL 60603
                                  312-443-3533
                                  Hours: Mon.-Fri. 10:30-4:30;
                                  Sat. 10-5; Sun. 12-5

Chicago's Art Institute is known world-wide for housing some of the greatest art ever created. After touring the Institute, be sure not to miss the gift shop. It has one of the most complete and outstanding collections of books about art and artists in Chicago. Many special Art Institute books highlight the past and present special exhibits at the museum.

In addition, they offer many reproductions of their famous paintings, framed and unframed, ready to adorn your walls at home. They also sell artistic jewelry, stationery, calendars, greeting cards, tote-bags, coffee mugs, T-shirts, and unique gifts. During Christmas they have a terrific selection of Christmas cards.

The Art Institute and gift shop are completely wheelchair accessible, but you will have to enter from the Columbus Drive East entrance. There is some limited handicapped parking available at that entrance. You can also use the Monroe Street underground parking. The gift shop is on the Michigan Avenue side of the museum.

The center court of the Art Institute is a delightful place for lunch while you tour the museum. The Goodman Theatre is also attached and is a well-known and acclaimed Chicago theatre.

If you're new to Chicago, you'll recognize the famous two lions on guard at the front steps of the Art Institute.

B. Dalton Bookseller

General   129 N. Wabash Ave.
                                    Chicago, IL 60602
                                    312-236-7615
                                    Hours: Mon.-Thurs. 9:30-7;
                                    Fri.-Sat. 9:30-6

It's every book lover's dream: 12,000 square feet of books. The dream comes true at B. Dalton Bookseller. Two stories of pure book-loving delight are linked by elevator and escalator. In trying to decide what departments are their specialties, I gave up. They all are complete.

In addition to special savings on a tremendous amount of discount books, B. Dalton has a Book Savers Club which allows a 10% discount at all B. Dalton Bookseller stores. Members receive a bi-monthly newsletter called "Just Browsing" that describes new releases and has additional coupons. There is a nominal fee for membership.

The club is just one way B. Dalton treats their customers as very special people. Each branch customizes their stock to meet the needs of their particular clientele. Corporate clients can open a B. Dalton Bookseller account and the store occasionally delivers books to corporations located near the Wabash store.

For the convenience of customers, B. Dalton leases space to Software Etc. There you'll find software, games, and computer books.

Purchases from this section must be paid for separately upon checkout. Hardly a drawback when you consider the convenience.

If you haven't the time to read a full book, B. Dalton dedicates one huge wall to over 600 magazine titles. Some are imports from Britain, France, Italy, Spain, and Germany. Another section that has been growing is audio tapes. They carry 400-500 book titles on tape. This section is especially strong in fiction, business, and self-help.

Authors visit the store for autographing sessions. B. Dalton prefers to concentrate on books instead of extra book-related merchandise; however they do have a supply of bookmarks, book covers, bookends, calendars, maps, games, and postcards.

Complete with an enthusiastic manager, B. Dalton Bookseller on North Wabash succeeds in providing quality stock and top-notch helpful employees. If they can't get you the book you want, it probably isn't in print.

B. Dalton Bookseller

General

175 W. Jackson
Chicago, IL 60604
312-922-5219
Hours: Mon.-Fri. 7:30-5:30

For wheelchair access, use the mall entrance.

B. Dalton Bookseller

General

645 N. Michigan Ave.
Chicago, IL 60611
312-944-3702
Hours: Mon.-Sat 10-6:30
Sun. 11-5

Barbara's Bookstore

General

1350 North Wells St.
Chicago, IL 60610
312-642-5044
Hours: Mon.-Sat. 10-10;
Sun. 11-8

Chicago Central

"We are passionate about books," says Pat Peterson, a co-owner of the Barbara's Bookstore "chainlet". Patrons are passionate about each of the four locations of Barbara's Bookstore.

"Although each Barbara's Bookstore takes great pride in responding directly to the immediate community it serves," Pat continued, "there are major similarities in philosophy, inventory, and operations at all four stores."

The similarities include top quality book selections and the friendliness of the employees who make the store feel like a second home for many patrons. Books for every interest are available at all of Barbara's branches. Each store is attractively designed for browsing and locating books when you're in a hurry. Topics include fiction, biography, mystery, literature, philosophy, travel and tourism, women's studies, gay issues, theatre, and local interest. Some books on audio tapes are available. A large selection of calendars are available during the fall.

They publish a newsletter which highlights the many services and special events. Services available at all of the Barbara's Bookstores include house charge accounts, free gift wrapping, shipping, phone orders, author autographing sessions, and recommendations.

At the branch on North Wells Street, they conduct frequent readings by nationally known authors and a children's story hour. The oldest of Barbara's Bookstores, this store was established in 1963. They stock approximately 60,000 copies of 25,000 different titles. The store is wheelchair accessible although inside about ten percent is not accessible.

Whether you are just visiting Chicago or you live here, you must visit Barbara's Bookstore. This is one of Chicago's best known bookstores.

The other branches are located at 3130 North Broadway and 1800 North Clybourn in Chicago and at 1110 Lake Street in Oak Park.

Beck's Book Store

Text, General

209 N. Wabash Avenue
Chicago, IL 60601
312-630-9113
Hours: Mon.-Thurs. 8-6;
Fri. 8-5; Sat. 8-1

This branch of Beck's Book Store supplies students at Harold Washington College with textbooks and school supplies. The book store is open to the public and is wheelchair accessible.

Booksellers Row

Used, Antiquarian

408 S. Michigan Avenue
Chicago, IL 60605
312-427-4242
Hours: Mon.-Sat. 10:30-10:30;
Sun. 12-8

Bookseller's Row operates this branch location at the Fine Arts Building offering 20,000 selections. This store is currently on two levels (with a third in the planning phase), making it difficult for wheelchair customers. However, the staff is eager to help and will retrieve books from the second floor for disabled patrons. The Michigan Avenue branch offers both new and used books.

(Also see the review written about the Bookseller's Row on North Lincoln Avenue.)

Carl Fischer Music Inc.

Music

312 S. Wabash Ave.
Chicago, IL 60604
312-427-6652
Hours: Mon.-Fri. 9-5:30; Sat. 9-5

When musicians in Chicago talk about Fischer, they are referring to Carl Fischer Music Inc.

With over 610,000 titles of sheet music, Carl Fischer is the world's largest supplier of printed sheet music. The business was established in 1872 and still grows stronger every year.

"If it's in print, we specialize in it," says Vice President/General Manager Gary Sigurdson.

The 40,000 square foot store is wheelchair accessible. If you're a book lover and music lover, you'll enjoy visiting Carl Fischer Music Inc.

Columbia College Bookstore

Text

623 S. Wabash Ave.
Chicago, IL 60605
312-663-1600
Hours: Mon.-Thurs. 9-4; Fri. 9-3

The Contract Design Center Bookshop

Decorating Arts

P.O. Box 3442
11-111 Merchandise Mart
Chicago, IL 60654
312-527-3509
Hours: Mon.-Fri. 9-5

Located in Chicago's Merchandise Mart, The Contract Design Center is the only bookstore in Chicago devoted solely to various aspects of design. A majority of the books are highly specialized interior design books but architecture, graphics and drawing books are also stocked. There are approximately 3,800 titles in stock.

In addition to interior design for the home, The Contract Design Center offers specialized titles such as: "Medical and Dental Space Planning for the 1990s," "Successful Restaurant Design," "Planning and Designing the Office Environment," and "Design for Hospitality" which discusses hotel and motel planning for wheelchair accessible rooms.

If you are more interested in design components, you'll find a wide variety of books here addressing upholstery styles, effective use of light, color power, and window covering styles.

The novice decorator may be interested in titles such as: "Gardens of America," "Manhattan Style," and "Decorative Painting for Children's Rooms."

The Contract Design Center Book, a division of Shelby Williams Industries, Inc., does publish a catalogue. When you purchase one book from the catalogue, you become a club member. Membership enables you to purchase at club prices which are considerably below publishers' list prices. You'll receive a newsletter and all promotional materials of the club. As a member you are under no obligation to purchase any more books and can cancel membership at any time.

Periodically, The Contract Design Center Bookshop sponsors author autographing sessions. The store's manager, Daniel Osborn, has received special training in the field and is delighted to help you find the selection that best suits your needs. Special orders are welcome. Students with current ID's are given a ten percent discount off regularly priced items.

Totally wheelchair accessible, the store operates in the Merchandise Mart, one of the most exuberant design hubs in all of Chicago.

Coopersmith's

General

900 N. Michigan
Chicago, IL 60611
312-337-0330
Hours: Mon.-Thurs. 10-7; Fri.
10-8; Sat. 10-7; Sun. noon-6

If you have ever visited any of the three Coopersmith's branches, you know that they have an outstanding book selection, beautiful gifts, comfortable atmosphere, and terrific customer service.

The largest of the three stores is located in Woodfield Mall in Schaumburg. The suburban Vernon Hills and North Michigan Avenue stores are smaller. See the description of the Schaumburg store for more details.

Crown Books

General

201 W. Jackson Blvd.
Chicago, IL 60606
312-341-0505
Hours: Mon.-Fri. 8-7;
Sat. 9-5

Crown Books

General

309 W. Washington
Chicago, IL 60606
312-346-8677
Hours: Mon.-Fri. 8-7;
Sat. 9-5

Crown Books

General

26 N. Wabash
Chicago, IL 60602
312-782-7667
Hours: Mon.-Fri. 9-7;
Sat. 9-6; Sun. 12-5

Doubleday Book Shop

General
435 E. Illinois St., North Pier
Chicago, IL 60611
312-222-2524
Hours: Mon.-Fri. 10-9;
Sat. 10-11; Sun. noon-6

Dr. William M. Scholl College of Podiatric Medicine

Podiatry, Text
1001 N. Dearborn
Chicago, IL 60610
312-280-2931 x2931
Hours: Mon.-Fri. 10-3

Feet are getting stepped on all the time and more and more people are taking their tired, beaten, worn dogs to a podiatrist. One of the most famous names related to podiatry, Dr. William Scholl, has a podiatry college in his name right here in Chicago. Where there is a college, a bookstore is always nearby.

"Our bookstore is primarily for use by students at Scholl College," said Julia Fabris, the bookstore co-ordinator. "However, the public is welcome and phone orders are accepted."

In addition to textbooks, the bookstore sells podiatric instruments and surgical clothing. The store is wheelchair accessible. Off-street parking is available and mass transit runs nearby.

Field Museum of History--Shop

History
Roosevelt Rd. &
Lake Shore Drive
Chicago, IL 60605
312-922-9410
Hours: Daily 9-5

When you visit the Field Museum of History you can enhance your visit by stopping at the museum's bookstore. You'll find 8,000 volumes that will increase your appreciation of the exhibits you saw.

Located at Roosevelt Road and Lake Shore Drive, the museum shop is open from 9 am until 5 pm daily. Members receive special discounts. Since the shop is located on the first floor, it is wheelchair accessible.

As a service to their patrons, museum shop workers arrange special events such as craft demonstrations and children's story telling. Call them to find out the times and dates these special events are conducted.

Book topics range from anthropology, archaeology, architecture, biography, and antiques, to travel, black studies, and horticulture. Many books are geared toward children. If the topic you would like to study is not available, the shop will special order books. Gifts with an accent on natural history are also available.

Harry L. Stern Ltd.

Antiquarian, ABAA

29 N. Wacker, Ste. 700
Chicago, IL 60606
312-372-0388
<u>Hours:</u> Appointment Only

A member of the Antiquarian Bookseller's Association of America, Harry L. Stern conducts his antiquarian book sales by appointment only. In addition to books about American history, Harry sells antique maps and illuminated manuscripts. He is well versed in the book industry and does appraisals.

I Love A Mystery Bookstore

Mystery

55 E. Washington
Chicago, IL 60602
312-236-1338
<u>Hours:</u> Mon.-Fri. 9:30-5

IIT Chicago Kent Law College Books

Law Texts

77 S. Wacker Dr.
Chicago, IL 60606
312-567-5018
<u>Hours:</u> Mon.-Fri. 11-6

Joined to the IIT Chicago Kent Law College, the bookstore's hours can vary according to the needs of students of the college. Their main emphasis is law textbooks but they do have study aids and other required books and miscellaneous supplies. The college teaches MBA programs and tax courses.

The bookstore will be moving to Adams & Clinton Streets so it is advisable to call before visiting the store.

John G. Shedd Aquarium Sea Shop

Marine Life

1200 S. Lake Shore Dr.
Chicago, IL 60605
312-939-2426
Hours: Daily 9:30-6

Whether you are visiting the Shedd Aquarium just to get ideas for designing your ten-gallon tank at home or because you believe the sea and oceans to be Earth's future, you'll find books in the Sea Shop of the John G. Shedd Aquarium that can answer your questions.

Like the aquarium itself, the Sea Shop is wheelchair accessible. Books on marine life are in stock for all ages. With their new whale residents, the Shedd Aquarium is a terrific place to take the kids.

Kroch's & Brentano's Inc.

General

516 N. Michigan Avenue
Chicago, IL 60611
312-321-0989
Hours: Mon.-Fri. 10-6; Sat.
10:30-5:30

Kroch's & Brentano's Inc.

General

230 South Clark
Chicago, IL 60604
312-553-0171
Hours: Mon.-Fri. 8-6

Kroch's & Brentano's Inc.

General

30 N. LaSalle Street
Chicago, IL 60602
312-704-0287
Hours: Mon.-Fri. 8-6

Kroch's & Brentano's Inc.

General

29 S. Wabash Ave.
Chicago, IL 60603
312-332-7500
Hours: Mon. & Thurs. 9-7;
Tues., Wed., Fri. 9-6; Sat. 9-6

Adolph Kroch, who founded his bookstore in 1907, would be proud to see the continued growth and top quality maintained in his store. In 1937 Brentano's was purchased and continued to expand through the decades by Adolph Kroch's son, Carl.

"Today, Kroch's and Brentano's, Inc. is an employee owned and operated full service bookstore offering broad selections and service in all general book areas with a special depth and expertise in art, business, and professional book fields," says William W. Rickman, President of Kroch's & Brentano's, Inc.

For generations, Kroch's & Brentano's has been pleasing their customers with excellent services: handling special orders at no extra cost, free gift-wrapping, out-of-print search service, mailing anywhere in the world, children's story telling times, craft demonstrations, author readings, and frequent author autographing sessions with the book world's top writers.

With access to more than 120,000 titles, Kroch's & Brentano's includes books published by university presses and small publishers. There are over a million volumes in stock in the South Wabash store. They have at least one dictionary in each of 89 different languages and dialects. A visit to this department constitutes a lesson in geography for everyone.

If you have visited any of the eighteen locations in the Chicago area, you know that Kroch's & Brentano's also sells unique gifts, games, puzzles, greeting cards, gift wraps, address books, organizers, calendars, and journals. Books on tape continue to grow in popularity and Kroch's & Brentano's answers clients' requests by keeping many in stock.

Patrons will often find tables of quality discounted books and the store extends discounts to corporations, libraries, and schools when quantities are purchased.

"Kroch's & Brentano's is pledged to continue to identify and serve Chicago's book needs as it has for generations," William Rickman added. "We feel no one anywhere offers a better selection of books that our customers may want to own."

Marshall Field & Company

General

111 N. State Street
Chicago, IL 60630
312-781-4284
Hours: Mon.,Thurs. 9:45-7;
Tues., Wed., Fri., Sat. 9:45-5:45

The ornate trademark clock outside tells you that you are stepping into a store rich with Chicago tradition, Marshall Field & Company. The Book Department contains general interest books, many beautiful for gift-giving. The children's selection and cookbooks offer particularly good selections.

The store sponsors many author-autographing sessions. Bestselling authors are sure to show up here.

Wheelchair accessibility is no problem.

Moody Bookstore

Religious

150 W. Chicago Ave.
Chicago, IL 60610
312-329-4352
Hours: Mon.-Sat. 8:45-5

Museum of Contemporary Art Store

Art

237 E. Ontario St.
Chicago, IL 60611
312-280-2679
Hours: Tues.-Sat. 10-5;
Sun. 12-5

National Louis University Bookstore

Text

18 S. Michigan Ave.
Chicago, IL 60603
312-621-9650 x2269
Hours: Call ahead

Operating in conjunction with Louis University, the bookstore carries textbooks, best sellers, school supplies, school imprinted merchandise, and computer discs. They carry approximately 300 titles and offer a 25% discount on best sellers. Other new and used books in stock address the fields of accounting, computers, psychology, social services, black studies, reference, travel and tourism, education, and women's studies.

At special times, the bookstore sponsors author autographing sessions. The store is wheelchair accessible with no stairs to complicate matters. Parking is available on the street and mass transit is close.

Prairie Avenue Bookshop

Architecture

711 S. Dearborn
Chicago, IL 60605
312-922-8311
Hours: Mon.-Fri. 9:30-5:30;
Sat. 10-4

The largest architectural bookstore in the United States is as close as 711 S. Dearborn in Chicago. Prairie Avenue Bookshop is proud of their selection of architectural books as well as the Frank Lloyd Wright stone lithographs available.

While most of the bookshop's 3,500 books are new, there are a few used books in stock. The store is not wheelchair accessible from the outside.

Psychology Book Store Inc.

Psychology

220 S. State
Chicago, IL 60605
312-341-3480
Hours: Mon.- Fri. noon-6

Psychiatrists, psychologists, and people who like to study the mind will find the Psychology Book Store a must. With the exclusive topic of psychology, the store offers new, used, graduate, and professional books. Over 3,000 titles are in stock.

The store plays talk shows from the radio and offers discounts. The store is wheelchair accessible with no stairs at the entrance. Street parking and mass transit are available.

Rand McNally Map Store

Maps

150 South Wacker
Chicago, IL 60606
312-332-2009
Hours: Mon.-Fri. 7:30-6;
Sat. 10-4

Rand McNally is wheelchair accessible through the back door. Call ahead to make arrangements or bring someone with you if you are wheelchair bound.

Rand McNally Map Store

Maps

444 North Michigan
Chicago, IL 60611
312-321-1751
Hours: Mon. & Thurs. 9-7;
Tues., Wed., Fri. 9-6;
Sat. 10-6; Sun. 12-5

Rand McNally is wheelchair accessible through the back door.

Redig's Book Market

General

6 E. Cedar
Chicago, IL 60611
312-944-3358
Hours: Mon.-Fri. 10:30-10;
Sat. 9:30-10pm; Sun. 10:30-8

Rizzoli Bookstore

General

3rd Level, Water Tower Place
Chicago, IL 60611
312-642-3500
Hours: Mon.-Sat. 10-10;
Sun. 11-6; holidays hours vary

One of Chicago's best loved bookstores is Rizzoli Bookstore. Established in 1976, the store now has 15,000 titles all of a general interest nature. The atmosphere of this store is wonderful. The wood paneling and architectural detailing make it attractive to the eye, and your sense of hearing will enjoy the great sound system.

Rizzoli Bookstore is particularly noted for their art sections and beautiful gift books. They also sell compact discs and musical cassette tapes, blank books with gorgeous covers, and a selection of stationery.

Experienced in book selling, employees are well versed and always ready to assist you. Special services are free gift wrapping, special orders, mail order, newsletters, author autographing, and live music at times. Rizzoli Bookstore publishes a beautiful catalogue of elegant gift books.

Rizzoli Bookstore is wheelchair accessible except for the music and stationery departments which are up sixteen steps. This beautiful bookstore is a popular one in Chicago. They also have a branch location in Oak Brook, which is equally attractive.

Robert Morris College Bookstore

Text

180 N. LaSalle
Chicago, IL 60601
312-836-4834
Hours: Mon., Tues., Thurs.
7:30-6; Wed. & Fri. 7:30-4

Roosevelt University Bookstore

Text

431 S. Wabash
Chicago, IL 60601
312-341-3592
Hours: Mon. & Tues., 9-6;
Wed. & Thurs. 9-5; Fri. 9-1

Saint Paul Book & Media Center

Religious

172 N. Michigan Ave.
Chicago, IL 60601
312-346-4228
Hours: Mon.-Fri. 9:30-5:30;
Sat. 9:30-5

A Catholic bookstore, Saint Paul Book & Media Center carries about 4,000 books, videotapes, music cassettes. Many books are printed in Spanish. Topics include biography, education, and religion.

The store is wheelchair accessible. Parking and mass transit are nearby. Saint Paul Book & Media Center publishes its own newsletter.

Sandmeyer's Bookstore in Printer's Row

General

714 S. Dearborn
Chicago, IL 60605
312-922-2104
Hours: Tues., Wed., Fri. 11-6:30;
Thurs. 11-8; Sat. 11-5; Sun. 12-5

Owners Ulrich and Ellen Sandmeyer welcome you to their attractive shop located in the historic district that housed Chicago's printing industry one hundred years ago. Now Printer's Row carries a neighborhood ambiance in a big city setting.

Over 13,000 new books are stocked in this open, airy bookstore. The Sandmeyers are particularly proud of their extensive section of travel books, fiction, and children's books. Many sale books are available and special orders are no problem.

In addition to books, Sandmeyer's sells cards, musical cassettes, and some children's toys and puzzles. Gift wrapping is available and they will ship books anywhere.

Located in an older building that does not accommodate wheelchairs, the entrance to Sandmeyer's Bookstore has three steps. Parking on the street and an off-street parking lot is available for a small fee. Mass transit is available.

The Savvy Traveller

Travel

50 E. Washington
Chicago, IL 60602
312-263-2100
Hours: Mon.-Sat. 10-6; Thurs.
10-7; extra hours during Xmas

Well travelled employees can help you find anything in The Savvy Traveller which is a specialized travel bookstore. Carrying over 7,000 travel books, The Savvy Traveller offers you much more than just books.

Monthly travel seminars are held at no charge, according to Sandye Wexler, manager. Not restricted to travelogues, seminars have been held about packing a suitcase, women's adventure tours, and travel writing. Experts conduct the seminars and talks usually last a little more than an hour. Newsletters are sent monthly to keep customers up-to-date about new books and the up-coming seminars.

"We define travel rather broadly," states Sandye. "We also sell photography books, maps, videos, and even fiction: anything that relates to travel. We try to stock everything a traveller needs for both enlightenment and physical and psychological comfort."

They sell a variety of travel gear: luggage carts, electricity and currency converters, travel umbrellas, travel diaries, and more. Sandye claims, "It's a one-stop shop for travellers."

If you are disabled, no problem. The Savvy Traveller is wheelchair accessible with regular and handicapped restrooms available. Plans include expanding to an upstairs floor and there is already an elevator operating. In addition, they carry a few travel books specifically aimed at the disabled traveller. Nearby public parking lots and mass transit accessibility make The Savvy Traveller easy to reach.

When you're ready to travel but can't afford airfare, head for The Savvy Traveler.

Science of Mind Bookshop

Metaphysics

Watertower Place, Ste. 913E
Chicago, IL 60611
312-337-3637
Hours: Mon.-Fri. 10-4:30

This bookstore is wheelchair accessible.

Stuart Brent Books

General

670 N. Michigan Ave.
Chicago, IL 60611
312-337-6357
Hours: Mon.-Fri. 9-7;
Sat. 9-6; Sun. 12-5

Saul Bellow once called Stuart Brent "the Orpheus of Chicago booksellers." Allan Bloom said, "Stuart Brent is more than Chicago's premier bookseller. For more than forty years he has been cheerleader and nurse of Chicago's writers." Throughout Stuart Brent's store, you'll find framed photographs of Mr. Brent with many of Chicago's famed writers including Ben Hecht, Studs Terkel, Jack Conroy, Robert Parrish, and Nelson Algren. Newspaper clippings praising his bookstore for the past 45 years can also be found. But don't just look at the walls. Chances are good that Mr. Brent will be in the store conducting business as usual. If he has a moment to greet you, you'll meet one of Chicago's famous people.

The bookstore is elegant and is located on two floors. Unfortunately, that makes the basement level impossible for wheelchairs to manage. The

store stocks between 70,000-100,000 general interest books. Fine art
books are a particular specialty.

Mr. Brent wrote a book titled "The Seven Stairs" which discusses his
experiences and philosophy of bookselling. The book has messages for
everyone involved with books: the publisher, the bookseller, the writer,
and the book lover. Written 25 years ago, it's still in print and available
in his store. If Mr. Brent is in the store, he'll be happy to autograph your
copy for you.

In "The Seven Stairs" Mr. Brent's talks about books: "In the modern
world, good reading offers one of the few means of getting back to one's
self, of refreshing the spirit, of relating to the inward life of man.
Through reading you can get acquainted all over again with yourself.
You can stand being alone. You will look forward again to tomorrow."

Terra Museum of American Art Books

Fine Art
666 N. Michigan Ave.
Chicago, IL 60611
312-664-3939
Hours: Tues. noon-8;
Wed.-Sat. 10-5; Sun. noon-5

You can enjoy the treasures of the Terra Museum of American Art
by visiting the bookstore and purchasing a book about fine art, antiques,
architecture and arts and crafts. Many of the books relate to the
Museum's exhibits. You'll receive a free poster with your purchase. Also
for sale are prints, notecards, and posters.

The store is wheelchair accessible. Garage parking and mass transit
are close by. Take time to enjoy the splendid artwork on display and be
sure to check out the bookstore.

US Catholic Bookstore

Religious
205 W. Monroe St.
Chicago, IL 60606
312-855-1908
Hours: Mon., Tues., Thurs., Fri.
9:30-5; Wed. 8-5

Sponsored by the Claretian Missionaries, US Catholic Bookstore
serves all faiths. The bookstore actually has divided it's 2,500 square feet
into three separate special areas.

The bookstore has 12,000 books with a scholarly, popular, and spiritual focus. They have a vast selection of Bibles, many in Spanish. Topics also address black studies, hispanic studies, native American studies, eastern Christian religions, and women's studies.

The second area of the store sells a tremendous selection of handmade gifts and arts and crafts items from many developing countries. The gifts can be religious or practical. From Central and South America are handbags, wood carvings, handpainted plaques, and pottery animals. From Africa are fine leather products. From Russia and Poland are delicate hand-painted eggs. Bavarian wax art objects (not candles), such as a 22-inch Madonna and child, are in stock. Also in the gift section are religious icons, both original and prints.

The third section of the bookstore is a meditation room where scripture study lunch programs are held twice weekly. Recovery Groups are conducted weekly. Sometimes you just need a quiet place for meditating and US Catholic Bookstore has provided just such a place.

The US Catholic Bookstore publishes the US Catholic and Salt magazines and various newsletters. The store is wheelchair accessible.

US Government Bookstore

General

219 S. Dearborn St., Room 1356
Chicago, IL 60604
312-353-5133
Hours: Mon.-Fri. 8:30-4

The government wants to give you something free. You don't believe it? Stop into the US Government Bookstore and you'll find hundreds of booklets about almost every subject you can imagine from health and housing to travel and hobbies.

A terrific selection of books printed by the US government is available for a fee. The catalogue is free. Many accessories are also available which makes learning easy for children. For example, you can purchase books about space travel and NASA decals commemorating many famous space missions. You'll find a huge selection of posters and photographs sure to add sparkle to a classroom or child's bedroom.

Do you like to relax with a magazine? Government Periodicals are available on a subscription basis and cover an incredible range of topics and all price ranges. Maybe you have something to sell to the government. The US Government Bookstore tells you how to sell to many branches of the government.

At the US Government Bookstore you'll have the assistance of the staff in helping you find just what you need. Discounts are given to bookstores and to anyone purchasing 100 or more copies of the same title.

Chicago Central

The store is wheelchair accessible and an elevator is available to get to the 13th floor bookstore location. Your best bet for parking is to find a nearby garage. Mass transit is available.

If you want to learn to speak Cantonese, name constellations in the northern sky, or read about the findings of the Advisory Panel on Alzheimer's Disease, the US Government Bookstore has the answers.

W. Graham Arader III

Art

620 N. Michigan Ave., Ste. 470
Chicago, IL 60611
312-337-6033
Hours: Mon., Wed., Sat. 10-6;
Thurs., Fri. 9-4

A specialist in art reference books, W. Graham Arader III also stocks botanical topics and books regarding birds. This branch of the chain is wheelchair accessible.

Waldenbooks

General

127 Madison St. & S. LaSalle
Chicago, IL 60602
312-236-8446
Hours: Mon.-Fri. 8:30-6

Waldenbooks

General

233 S. Wacker Drive
Chicago, IL 60606
312-876-0308
Hours: Mon.-Fri. 8-5:30;
Sat. 10-5:30

Williams-Sonoma

Cooking

17 E. Chestnut St.
Chicago, IL 60611
312-642-1593
<u>Hours:</u> Mon., Tues., Wed., Fri.
10-6; Thurs. 10-7; Sat. 10-5:30;
Sun. 12-4

The Williams-Sonoma name should make your taste buds tingle. They specialize in gourmet cooking and have the books and cookware to achieve any wizardry you can create in your kitchen.

The store does have four steps to enter making wheelchairs entry impossible.

Chicago North

Act I Bookstore

Performing Arts

2632 North Lincoln
Chicago, IL 60614
312-348-6757
Hours: Mon.-Thurs. 10-8;
Fri. & Sat. 10-6; Sun. 12-6

Everyone in Chicago who loves the theatre will thoroughly enjoy visiting Act I Bookstore. This small store has a tremendous selection of books about the acting profession, stage make-up, characterization, directing know-how, biographies, children on stage, overcoming stage fright, theatre history, Shakespeare, magazines, and an incredible group of plays both in actor's editions and for the reader's enjoyment. Most books are new but a few shelves are devoted to old books that sell for twenty-five cents each.

At the front door is a bulletin board filled with information about auditions. They also sell T-shirts that list all of the theatres in Chicagoland. There is one step to enter the store but it is manageable and completely accessible inside.

If you have a love for the theatre, you'll love this specialized bookstore. You can learn to be a star at Act I.

Aspidistra Bookshop

Used

2630 N. Clark
Chicago, IL 60614
312-549-3129
Hours: Mon.-Thurs. 11-9;
Fri. 11-10; Sat. 11-9;
Sun. 12-7:30

Even if you really don't like used books, when you visit Aspidistra Bookshop, you'll be converted. The quality of the books is tremendous and the number of titles overwhelming. Both paper and hardbacks are available in a general interest theme. Topics include history, fiction, reference, scholarly, biography, foreign countries, poetry, business, scientific, humor, and so much more. The store is also interested in buying books. For the collector, Aspidistra Bookshop has some rare and antique books in the front case.

There are no steps to enter the store making it an easy one to enter. The aisles are narrow but manageable. There are only a few aisles that are too close to maneuver. The store has plenty of patrons and workers who are helpful in retrieving books from top shelves.

Aspidistra Bookshop was established in 1972 and has been a popular book hot spot since then. Parking is almost impossible to find on the street but that doesn't deter anyone. Use mass transit or find a parking garage. The store is always busy with old friends and newcomers who usually exclaim in excitement as they find books they thought had disappeared long ago.

Whatever your budget, you'll enjoy choosing books from this collection. Whatever your interest, you'll find it at Aspidistra Bookshop.

Aurum Solis Occult

Metaphysics

5142 N. Clark
Chicago, IL 60640
312-334-2120
Hours: Mon. & Tues. 11-7;
Wed.-Sat. 11-8; Sun. noon-5

In Latin Aurum Solis means "Golden Sun". Aurum Solis is a metaphysical bookstore that was established two years ago. All 2,000 titles in the store highlight metaphysics, occult, New Age, philosophy, comparative religion, and even Carl Jung. The store also publishes a catalogue featuring 8,000 more titles.

In addition to books, Aurum Solis rents video tapes relating to metaphysics and sells music, incense, magazines, and other assorted items.

The store has one six inch high step at the entrance; many people using wheelchairs will need some assistance. The store is wheelchair accessible within.

Barbara's Bookstore

General

3130 N. Broadway
Chicago, IL 60657
312-477-0411
Hours: Mon.-Fri. 10am-10pm;
Sat. 10-9; Sun. 11-10

Well-known in Chicago, this branch of Barbara's Bookstore was established in 1971. They stock 27,000 different titles and have 65,000 books in stock. The store is totally wheelchair accessible. Be sure to purchase your literary T-shirt at this branch.

See the full write-up describing all of the Barbara's Bookstores in the Chicago Central chapter of *The Book Lover's Guide to Chicagoland*.

Barbara's Bookstore

General

1800 N. Clybourn
Chicago, IL 60614
312-664-1113
Hours: Mon.-Thurs. 10-9; Fri. &
Sat. 10-11pm; Sun. 11-8

This newest branch of Barbara's Bookstore was established in 1990. They stock 20,000 different titles and have 40,000 books in stock. The children's department is particularly strong and not to be missed. The store is totally wheelchair accessible.

See the full write-up describing all of the Barbara's Bookstores in the Chicago Central chapter of *The Book Lover's Guide to Chicagoland*.

Beasley Books

Antiquarian, ABAA

1533 W. Oakdale
Chicago, IL 60657
312-472-4528
Hours: Appointment and mail
order

As members of the Antiquarian Booksellers Association of America, Elizabeth and Paul Garon, who own Beasley Books, focus their collection on modern first editions, radical literature, African-American literature, jazz and blues, detective fiction, and science fiction. Their business is conducted by appointment only. Catalogues are available. In stock are 3,000-4,000 titles.

Beck's Book Store

Text, General

113 Pearson
Chicago, IL 60610
312-944-7685
Hours: Mon.-Thurs. 8-6;
Fri. 8-4; Sat. 8-1

This branch of Beck's Book Store provides textbooks and supplies for students of Loyola/Mallinckrodt College. It is also open to the public and wheelchair accessible.

Beck's Book Store

Text, General

1125 W. Loyola Avenue
Chicago, IL 60626
312-743-2281
Hours: Mon.-Thurs. 8-6;
Fri. 8-5; Sat. 9-1

This branch of Beck's Book Store provides textbooks and supplies for students of Loyola University.

Beck's Book Store

Text, General

5500 N. St. Louis Avenue
Chicago, IL 60625
312-588-2770
Hours: Mon.-Thurs. 8:30-7;
Fri. 8:30-3

Associated with Northeastern Illinois University, Beck's Book Store on St. Louis Avenue is one of six branches in Chicago. The stores are open to the public even though most titles are stocked at the specific requests of professors. Office supplies and children's books are also available.

Beck's Book Store

Text, General   4520 N. Broadway
                                          Chicago, IL 60640
                                          312-784-7963
                                          Hours: Mon.-Thurs. 8-6;
                                          Fri. 8-5; Sat. 8-1

Beck's Book Store recently opened their sixth store. All are associated with colleges and carry textbooks specific to the colleges' needs and those books that professors have recommended as supplementary study. In addition they carry college and office supplies and stock children's books.

All the stores are open to the public and accessible to wheelchairs. Parking and mass transit are near each location.

The headquarters is at the 4520 N. Broadway address, which serves Truman College.

Bell, Book, & Candle

Metaphysics   5246 N. Clark
                                          Chicago, IL 60640
                                          312-878-7575
                                          Hours: Mon.-Sat. 11-6;
                                          Sun. 12-4

Good music and good conversation are just two of the many attributes that this bookstore has. Over 1,000 titles on metaphysics, occult, astrology, ritual magic, herbalism, Tao, Zen, and Christian literature are stocked. They also have a full line of herbs, oils, chalices, candles, rock crystal, jewelry, Tarot cards, and musical tapes.

The store is wheelchair accessible. Bell, Book, & Candle was established Christmas week in 1990 and is owned by Harley Macmillen.

Book Adventures

Used   3705 N. Southport
                                          Chicago, IL 60613
                                          312-477-4725
                                          Hours: Mon.-Fri. 5pm-mdnt.;
                                          Sat. & Sun. 2pm-mdnt.;
                                          (call to confirm)

Owner Mark R. Harris describes the used books in Book Adventures as "rediscovered and unusual books (fiction and nonfiction)." In addition to stocking over 10,000 used books, he carries offbeat periodicals and "zines."

The store is located three doors from the Music Box Theater in Chicago. It is wheelchair accessible and seating is available for the comfort of patrons.

Mark recommends that customers call to confirm hours before visiting since this is a one-person business. There may be only one person in the store but there are many heartbeats. The store has a collection of animals in residence. Pets include a dog, a cat, a potbelly pig, a parrot, and a pair of ferrets.

Book Box -- Shake, Rattle & Read

Used

4812 N. Broadway
Chicago, IL 60640
312-334-5311
Hours: Mon.-Thurs. 11-6;
Fri., Sat. 11-7; Sun. 12-6

For twenty-six years, people have been shaking, rattling, and reading books from this delightful book store. All of the estimated 60,000 books are used and most focus on the entertainment industry. There are many back issues of Hollywood and Rock magazines. As an added sideline, the store sells used records, cassettes, and compact discs. Rolling Stone voted Shake, Rattle, and Read as "the best browsing in Chicago." A surprising specialty is cookbooks.

The store is wheelchair accessible and you are sure to enjoy every inch of their 1,200 square feet. Owner Ric Addy has recently opened a "hip culture" store called Rave that is also listed in *The Book Lover's Guide*.

Booklegger's

Antiquarian

2935 N. Broadway
Chicago, IL 60657
312-404-8780
Hours: Open every day; times
vary during the year, call,
usually noon-6pm

Booklegger's airy store stocks 10-12,000 books in excellent condition about fine art, literary classics, Americana, philosophy, and contemporary fiction. Many books are first editions signed by the author. Beautiful art books are ready to land on your coffee table.

The store is completely wheelchair accessible. The hours of operation change seasonally.

Bookman's Corner

Used

2959 N. Clark
Chicago, IL 60657
312-929-8298
Hours: Mon.-Fri. noon-8;
Sat. noon-8; Sun. noon-6

On the sign outside the store, Bookman's Corner says they have "rare, medium, and well-done books." And the sign is right. Whatever your taste in used books, Bookman's Corner is sure to have something to calm your sweet tooth or spice up your reading time. Many used booksellers shop at Bookman's Corner. The shelves are astonishingly tall and the selections are terrific.

A wheelchair can get into Bookman's Corner with assistance but can't move very far inside since books piled everywhere makes aisles impossibly narrow. This is a delightful store where you'll never know what you'll find. Something here is certainly destined for your shelves.

Books Off Berwyn

General

5220 N. Clark
Chicago, IL 60640
312-878-9800
Hours: Mon.-Fri. 10-6:30;
Sat. 10-6; Sun. 10-4

Books off Berwyn used to be know as Books on Berwyn but now that they have moved, their new name is much more appropriate. The store has grown capacity and will be soon (if it hasn't already) extending into the store next door. The expansion will allow the store to further increase it's inventory as well as break into some other fields.

If you're not familiar with Dover Publications, you must check out Books off Berwyn. They stock all of Dover's massive inventory which makes it much easier for you to find exactly what you need rather than relying on a catalogue's description of available books. The selection is incredible. Dover published many books that are no longer being printed by the original publishers but are still in demand. They recently began a classics section where you can buy a classic for one dollar. Don't give quality a second thought. All Dover paperback books are softbound on acid free paper (which means they will never yellow with age) and stitched (which means their bindings won't break.) Dover books are top quality books at reasonable prices.

Books off Berwyn employees are happy to help you find the Dover Publication that meets your specific needs. For desktop publishers, Dover is a dream. Most of the art books have copyright free designs, illustrations, and decorative borders. Some books even have the non-reproducible blue lay-out lines for putting together flyers. For the musician, they publish musical scores, many of which are difficult to find. Books off Berwyn also stocks musical cassette tapes and compact discs to complement the book selections relating to music. For the artist, they have books about artists as well as how to create your own art work. Many books focus on architecture. Needleworkers find dozens of books to keep them busy from cross-stitch and crocheting, to iron-on decals to make clothing one-of-a-kind.

Children's activity books continue to give kids enjoyment. The selection of books cover a spectrum of interests. Kids make small cardboard castles, cut-out paper dolls, color in oversized coloring books, decorate the house with seasonal stencils, and even learn a few things from their Dover books.

The store has a slight incline to enter. Aisles and corners are really tight for wheelchairs but employees are happy to retrieve books that you may not be able to reach.

Books off Berwyn just celebrated their third year of business. With the growth they are experiencing, they must be selling books just right. This is a fun place to find books that you usually can't find on book shelves.

Books on Belmont

General

614 W. Belmont
Chicago, IL 60657
312-528-2665
Hours: Mon.-Fri. 1-9;
Sat. 1-8; Sun. 12-6

Books on Belmont stocks over 10,000 new and used books including architecture, history, metaphysics, fine art, gay issues, literature, occult, philosophy, women's studies and photography. Also for sale are records. Discounts are offered during sales at different times of the year.

The store has three steps to enter presenting a barrier to wheelchairs. Inside, the store is wheelchair accessible.

Booksellers Row

Used, Antiquarian

2445 N. Lincoln Ave.
Chicago, IL 60614
312-348-1170
<u>Hours:</u> Daily 11-10:30pm

Stepping inside Bookseller's Row on North Lincoln, book lovers know they're in paradise. Many of the books are review copies. Virtually all topics are covered and books are reasonably priced.

Lined with beautiful wooden shelves complete with tall rolling ladders, the store is fresh, airy and comfortably inviting. The friendly staff is always ready to answer a question or climb the ladders to reach that special selection.

Bookseller's Row stocks over 30,000 titles of used books and ornate antiquarian books covering literature, cinema, theatre, women's studies, biographies, history, computers, mystery, psychology and social sciences. They specialize in fine art books appropriate for your bookcase or coffee table.

The children's section is appropriate for the pint-sized. Lower shelves and kid-size chairs decorate the corner.

Owners Howard and Alison Cohen made sure that the Lincoln Avenue Bookseller's Row is completely wheelchair accessible and comfortable for everyone.

Whether you must take mass transit, drive your car, or skydive from an airplane be sure to get to Bookseller's Row. When you finish shopping, cross the street and step into The Red Lion, a traditional British pub complete with imported ales and outstanding British food. The combination of Bookseller's Row and The Red Lion Pub make for an entertaining Sunday afternoon.

(Also see the review of the branch Bookseller's Row on South Michigan Ave.)

The Bookworks

Antiquarian

3444 N. Clark
Chicago, IL 60657
312-871-5318
<u>Hours:</u> Mon.-Sat. 1pm-10;
Sun. noon-6

"We enjoy selling books," Bob Roschke, proprietor of The Bookworks on North Clark in Chicago, simply said. His enjoyment in the hunt for antiquarian books means clients find treasures in just one stop:

at the Bookworks. Bob once stumbled upon a first edition work by Charles Dickens.

Top quality rare and used books are well-organized and cover a broad subject selection. Prices are reasonable. New books by popular authors are also sold at the store. He currently carries approximately 40,000 books.

Bob is also interested in buying your books. He's always happy to offer cash or credit for better used or rare books. The quality of the book as well as the author is important to the antiquarian. Of today's authors, Bob predicts that Stephen King's first edition books will be extremely valuable. Some of King's earlier novels are already considered collectors' items.

Also for sale at The Bookworks are used and rare L.P. records, cassette tapes, vintage photographs, postcards, advertising and miscellaneous ephemera. Ephemera are items that are not intended to last and are passed out to the public, such as pamphlets, scorecards, notebooks, etc.

The Bookworks is completely wheelchair accessible. A parking lot is located behind the building. Mass transit is nearby.

"If something's been published, there's someone who's interested," said Bob in a recent issue of Chicago Tribune Magazine.

You must visit The Bookworks and you're sure to find just the book you have been looking for. Bob makes it easy for you: he does the heavy-duty digging while you can casually browse the shelves.

Chicago Historical Society Museum Books

Chicago   Clark St. at North Ave.
                                               Chicago, IL 60614
                                               312-642-4600
                                               Hours: Mon.-Sat. 9:30-4:30;
                                               Sun. noon-5

The bookstore at the Chicago Historical Society specializes in Chicago today and yesterday. They also carry an extensive selection of Civil War literature, books about ethnic groups in Chicago, and architecture, biography and social sciences. In stock you'll find jewelry, postcards, stationery, paper dolls, T-shirts, coffee mugs, and a full gift line of history related products. In November, 1991, the store conducted the First Annual Children's History Book Week.

Museum members are offered a 10% discount in the bookstore. Periodically, the bookstore conducts author autographing and children's story-telling sessions.

Located at Clark Street and North Avenue, the museum is open to anyone interested in Chicago's history. After walking down Chicago's Memory Lane, be sure to visit the bookstore. It's wheelchair accessible and open seven days per week. If you're looking for a special Chicago gift to keep or send to someone, be sure to visit the Chicago Historical Society's bookstore.

The Children's Bookstore

Children's

2465 N. Lincoln Ave.
Chicago, IL 60614
312-248-2665
Hours: Mon.-Wed. 10-8;
Thurs.-Sat. 10-10; Sun. 11-7

"Everyone who works here is a children's literature expert," says Andrew Laties of The Children's Bookstore. Located on Lincoln Avenue amidst a group of bookstores, your kids will enjoy this delightful store.

The Children's Bookstore sponsors a wide variety of special events including live music, author autographing, and even live theater. Four times per week the store has a special story-telling time. There is a large play area near the back of the store. All the books in stock are new and a few are written in French and Spanish. Parents will enjoy browsing in the child care section while the kids enjoy choosing books, book related toys, and audiotapes. The store has over 20,000 titles in stock.

"We sub-specialize in science and multicultural children's literature," Andrew added.

Discounts are given to schools and institutions. The Children's Bookstore attends many of the book fairs in the Chicagoland area. They will also go to schools and hospitals and set up a book fair of their own.

The store is wheelchair accessible. It is a bright, friendly atmosphere which encourages children to read.

Crown Books

General

2711 N. Clark St.
Chicago, IL 60614
312-327-1551
Hours: Mon.-Fri. 10-9;
Sat.-Sun. 10-6

Crown Books

General

1660 N. Wells St.
Chicago, IL 60614
312-642-3950
Hours: Mon.-Thurs. 10-9;
Fri.-Sat. 10-11; Sun. 10-6

Unlike most locations in the Crown Books chain, this location is not
wheelchair accessible.

Dan Behnke, Bookseller

Used

2463 N. Lincoln Ave.
Chicago, IL 60614
312-404-0403
Hours: Mon.-Sat. noon-10:30pm;
Sunday noon-7

Dan Behnke knows books. With 18,000 titles in stock, he operates an
attractive, airy store filled with quality used and out-of-print books.
"From time-to-time when collections are purchased a particular
category might be particularly strong," says Dan. "This has happened in
the past in the areas of children's books, military, architecture, history,
and sports."
Dan has computerized his business. He has a database of his stock
and can tell patrons if he has the book or not in mere seconds. He also
does searches for books patrons would like to purchase.
The store is wheelchair accessible and the stock is well organized.

DePaul University Bookstore

Text

2419 N. Sheffield
Chicago, IL 60614
312-341-8423
Hours: Mon.-Thurs. 9-6;
Fri. 9-5; Sat. 10-4: Summer:
Mon.-Fri. 9-5; Sat. 10-4

At the DePaul University Bookstore you'll find new and used
textbooks plus trade and mass-market books, DePaul clothing, gifts, cards
and calendars. The store is open to the general public even though it's
primarily intended as a service for DePaul students.

Fiery Clock Face

Used

5311 N. Clark
Chicago, IL 60640
312-728-4227
Hours: Tues.-Sun. 10-6

Looking for the right antique bookends to display your beautiful historic books? Check at The Fiery Clock Face on North Clark Street.

If you love antiques, this store is loaded with them. The atmosphere is old and quaint. The book selection consists of used books with a focus on children's books and cookbooks. I was delighted to find a good selection of Irish books: pretty picture books, Irish traditions, and old travel booklets. They also carry assorted old magazines in excellent condition, along with Illinois memorabilia and a few records.

It's a small store. Stand in the middle of the store and look around to notice all the pieces of artwork. The children's section has a variety of old toys.

The store is tight and it is difficult for a wheelchair to comfortably maneuver farther than the center aisle.

Grand Tour World Travel Bookstore

Travel

3229 N. Clark
Chicago, IL 60657
312-929-1836
Hours: Mon.-Sat. 10-10;
Sun. 11-7

You can travel the world without leaving Chicago at Grand Tour World Travel Book Store. The well-traveled owner, Bob Katzman, has collected a vast array of travel books describing over 150 countries, each of the 50 states, over 70 foreign language dictionaries, 300 different maps, 150 flags from foreign countries along with posters, bookmarks, flyers, and even some international brands of cigarettes.

His philosophy of "make it" extends to the physical aspects of Grand Tour World Travel Bookstore as well. Bob himself made the bookcases and main counter in the store.

"Because I've traveled extensively all over America and Europe myself," Bob said, "I'm able to suggest places for people to travel. The other day I helped a woman choose a white-water rafting vacation in Wisconsin."

Sadly, the Grand Tour World Travel Bookstore is not designed for wheelchair accessibility. A chair can enter from the street but once inside, the person is faced with three steps.

Conveniently open seven days per week, Grand Tour World Travel Bookstore has off street parking available as well as close mass transit.

As a special bonus, Grand Tour World Travel Bookstore offers travel agents and teachers with identification a 10% discount off before sale prices.

When you don't have time to leave Chicago, the next best thing is visiting The Grand Tour World Travel Bookstore.

Guild Books

General

2456 N. Lincoln Ave.
Chicago, IL 60614
312-525-3667
Hours: Mon.-Sat. 11-10:30pm;
Sun. noon-10:30pm

"We're a cultural center as much as a bookstore, a specialist in literature, politics and theatre," says Lew Rosenbaum, manager of Guild Books on North Lincoln Avenue. "We emphasize our community involvement, as with activities highlighting the creative contributions of homeless writers and artists."

Over 30,000 book titles in stock focus on politics, current affairs, theatre, and poetry. They also offer a tremendous selection of magazines available in English and foreign languages. You'll find the "Illustrated London News" and "Yoga Journal" next to magazines written in Arabic, French, Spanish, and many others.

A wide variety of Marxist and Leninist books are available. You'll even find a copy of Mao Tse-Tung's works written in Spanish. Other selections include novels written by Latin American, African-American, Asian, and African writers.

The store effectively utilizes 2,000 square feet and is wheelchair accessible with the exception of the health, philosophy and psychology sections. Those are up four steps. Narrow aisles are sometimes blocked with footstools but friendly employees and patrons help overcome this minor dilemma.

Since Guild Books pays attention to community activities, a bulletin board is located just inside the front door of Guild Books and carries flyers about theatre auditions in the city.

J. Toguri Mercantile Co.

Oriental   851 W. Belmont Ave.
                                               Chicago, IL 60657
                                               312-929-3500
                                               Hours: Mon.-Sat. 10-6

The Japanese sun shines at the J. Toguri Mercantile Company. In addition to the 6,500 volumes in stock, you'll enjoy browsing through the oriental art and craft items. Books available give detailed instructions about making the art and craft items yourself.

Other books describe the fine art of oriental home decorating and the ancient art of origami (paper folding). Have you ever wanted to grow bonsai miniature trees or play centuries old games such as Mah Jong, Shogi, or Go? You'll find just what you need and have the assistance of knowledgeable staff. Books discussing the popular martial arts of Judo, Karate, Aikido and Tai-Chi are big sellers.

Most of the books and magazines are written in Japanese but many English translations are available. You can also learn of Japanese activities in Chicagoland.

Macrobiotics is the latest nutritional craze and J. Toguri brings you books about the diets, Japanese style. If you need to get rid of pain and stress, read about Shiatsu acupressure.

The shop sells a variety of oriental wares: chinaware, lacquer ware, paper ware, dry goods, painting and floral design goods, kitchen ware and even non-perishable foods.

The J. Toguri Mercantile Company is wheelchair accessible, both inside and from the outside. The staff provides chairs for those people who need to take a bit of a rest while browsing.

If, by some remote chance, you can't find the book you're looking for on their shelves, they will special order books directly from Japan. If you're Japanese or simply an admirer of fine Japanese arts, you'll enjoy spending hours at the J. Toguri Mercantile Company. Established in 1944, the store continues to delight.

Kroch's & Brentano's Inc.

General   2070 N. Clybourn
                                               Chicago, IL 60614
                                               312-525-9123
                                               Hours: Mon.-Fri. 10-9; Sat. 10-6;
                                               Sun. noon-5

Larry Law's Bookstore

Mail order

831 Cornelia
Chicago, IL 60657
312-477-9247
Hours: Mail order and
appointment only

An interesting place to visit, Larry Law's Bookstore stocks over 5,000 titles covering theatre, cinema, ballet, Chicago, and World War II. Larry says he's interested in anything to do with World War II and is always interested in purchasing anything historical.

Also included for sale is a collection of ephemera from World Fairs and Expositions, coins, postcards, stamps, and videos. The business is conducted by appointment, phone, or mail order. A catalogue is available.

The Mustard Seed Christian Bookstore

Religious

1143 W. Sheridan Rd.
Chicago, IL 60660
312-973-7055
Hours: Mon.-Sat. 9:30-6:30

"The Mustard Seed Christian Bookstore is dedicated to being an ecumenical book source for the Christian market with emphasis in pastoral resource material in such areas as psychology and counseling for those in the ministry," says Philip Bujnowski, owner.

In addition to Christian literature and ministry counseling, the store carries a complete line of Bibles, along with books addressing recovery and addiction, social issues, orthodox spirituality and saints. There are over 8,000 titles on the shelves. You'll find greeting cards, Christian jewelry and music, gift plaques, Bible covers, wall crosses and a variety of religious articles. Another service offered is Bible imprinting.

Discounts are extended to institutions and churches. Mass transit is close. Wheelchair accessibility is no problem.

Mystery Loves Company

Mystery

3338 N. Southport Ave.
Chicago, IL 60657
312-935-1000
Hours: Tues.-Fri 10-6:30;
Sat. 10-5:30; Sun. noon-4

This mystery bookstore loves your company and concentrates on customer service. Established in 1989, the store has between 4-5,000 books all focusing on mystery, espionage, horror, and true crime. They publish a monthly newsletter and also sell games with a mystery theme.

There is one step at the front door but the store is wheelchair accessible within.

The Occult Bookstore

Magic, Occult

3230 N. Clark St.
Chicago, IL 60657
312-281-0599
Hours: Mon.-Thurs. 11-7;
Fri. & Sat. 11-9; Sun. noon-6

A truly unique store, The Occult Bookstore has been operating in Chicago since 1920. The books cover a range of topics including magic, astrology, meditation, yoga, eastern religions, numerology, psychic development and ancient Egyptian religion.

For the convenience of clients, The Occult Bookstore has an in-house palmist who reads Tarot cards. But if you would like to do your own Tarot card reading, you can select your deck from over 100 selections. By appointment, the store arranges for clients to have their astrological charts read. They also sell candles, incense, jewelry, and oils.

The store is not wheelchair accessible because there is one step at the entrance.

Pathfinder Bookstore

Metaphysical

1925 W. Thome Ave.
Chicago, IL 60660
312-262-3888
Hours: Mon.-Thurs. 10-9;
Fri. 10-5; Sat. & Sun. 10-6

A metaphysical bookstore that also carries self-help, healing, and spiritual books, Pathfinder Bookstore has been in business for ten years. They also stock gifts, greeting cards, charms, and incense. The store is wheelchair accessible.

Paul Rohe & Sons Booksellers

Used, Antiquarian

3176 N. Clark St.
Chicago, IL 60657
312-477-1999
Hours: Mon.-Sat. noon-9;
Sun. noon-6

Established in 1976, Paul Rohe and Sons Booksellers has a store filled with more than 50,000 books. Topics are broad and divided into 30-40 different categories. They stock a large selection of plays. The store has one step to enter but is manageable for wheelchairs that can do wheelies. The 1400 square feet within the store is wheelchair accessible.

People Like Us Books

Gay & Lesbian

3321 N. Clark St.
Chicago, IL 60657
312-248-6363
Hours: Daily 10-9

Co-owned by a gay man and a lesbian, People Like Us is more than just a bookstore presenting exclusively gay and lesbian literature. They are active in the community by contributing books to the Horizons Youth Group, donating funds to Gerber-Hart Library as well as contributing to other organizations within the gay and lesbian community. A bulletin board in the store describes community information of events and ticket sales.

Their summer 1991 newsletter described another role they serve: "We get so many questions from out-of-towners about where to go, what to do, etc...that sometimes we are gay concierges, and that's just one fact of bookselling. If you ever need any community information or book advice, just give us a ring."

In addition to 8-10,000 titles of books, People Like Us sells T-shirts, buttons, music, flags, games, posters, postcards, stickers, and magazines. The staff will special order books and soon will form their own members discount club. Currently, discounts are extended to Gerber-Hart Library members and N.A.M.E. members.

Chicago North

The store has two steps to enter but aisles inside are wheelchair accessible. Mass transit is close and street parking is available if you're lucky.

Established in 1988, People Like Us is involved in much more than just book selling. The owners state that they "feel that it is important to expose gay men to lesbian work and vice-versa. We do a lot of cross selling of titles (i.e. men's books to women) and this helps to expand the awareness of the gay and lesbian community as a whole."

Powell's Bookstore

Used

2850 N. Lincoln
Chicago, IL 60657
312-248-1444
Hours: Mon.-Fri. & Sun. 11-9;
Sat. 11-10

George, a friend who really knows books, recommends Powell's Bookstore on North Lincoln as his favorite bookstore. There are many good reasons to take this recommendation seriously.

The newest of the three Powell's Bookstore branches, this location on North Lincoln is actually three store fronts large. Currently, 8,000 square feet are filled with used books in a wide range of general interest books. They have outstanding selections in fiction, scholarly topics, fine art, photography, architecture, cookbooks, and thousands of children's books. They are all great bargains and reflect the demographics of the book lovers in the Lincoln Park/Lakeview area. The custom-made wooden bookcases extend to the top of the old-fashioned high ceilings. With wider aisles than the 57th Street branch, this store is much more accessible for wheelchairs and has an airy feeling for the more claustrophobic clients.

One section of the store is in a completely separate room devoted to rare antiquarian books. Most selections here are about fine art, architecture, and books about books. The remaining 2,000 square feet is destined to become retail space. Since Powell's Bookstore has renovated the store, many new restaurants and gourmet deli's have moved into the area. Fortunately, Powell's Bookstore has the versatility, resources, and space to continue their development.

If you have the chance, be sure to stop here. Tell them George sent you.

Rave

Hip Culture

3730 N. Clark
Chicago, IL 60613
312-549-2325
Hours: Tues.-Thurs. noon-mdnt.;
Fri. & Sat. noon-2am;
Sun. 2pm-8pm

Connected to a nightclub, the 2,000 books stocked at Rave are mostly research books about "hip culture" chosen by owner Ric Addy. Rock magazines from Europe are for sale. Rave is primarily devoted to selling compact discs and cassettes of rock and alternative music. Ric says he stocks many of the musicians played on college radio.

The store is wheelchair accessible and open late night hours for the convenience of the nightclub crowd. For all the books that are the current rage, visit Rave.

Revolution Books

Revolutionary

3449 N. Sheffield
Chicago, IL 60657
312-528-5353
Hours: Wed.-Fri. 4pm-8pm;
Thurs. 2pm-7pm; Sat. noon-6;
Sun. noon-4

You say you want a revolution? Check out the collection of books at Revolution Books to review the progressive, radical, and revolutionary books about philosophy, history, economics, fiction, women's studies, and black studies. They also sell literature from the Revolutionary Communist Party U.S.A. Some books available are foreign imports. Other merchandise includes T-shirts and buttons.

Richard Cady Rare Books

Antiquarian

312-944-0856
Hours: Appointment only

A true book lover himself, Richard Cady sells select rare antiquarian books. He occasionally has a book or two from the 15th or 16th centuries but his focus is English and American literature from fine presses. Many of the books have exquisite bindings and are autographed by the author. He also has an interest in books about books and chooses quite a few of these for his collection of 2,000 books. Illustrated books and first editions are also of interest to him. The cost of the books he sells starts at $25.00 and goes up from there.

In addition to books, he has posters and book art pieces all relating to books and book selling. Many literary autographs are a part of his collection.

A book lover since childhood, Richard has been involved in book selling for twenty-five years. He established his own business in October of 1980. His business runs by appointment only and he does publish a catalogue.

Scenes Coffeehouse & Drama Bookstore

Performing Arts   3168 N. Clark St.
Chicago, IL 60657
312-525-1007
Hours: Sat. 9am-1am;
Mon-Thurs. 8:30am-12mdnt;
Fri. 8:30am-1am;

Catering to everyone, not just artists and actors, Scenes Coffeehouse & Drama Bookstore is one of Chicago's unique bookstores.

"We encourage a relaxed, friendly atmosphere where people can enjoy a cup of coffee and conversation with old friends," is how manager Kenn L. D. Frandsen describes the store.

In stock are over 3,000 books and magazines about theatre, plays, theatre management, fiction, cinema, performing art, literature, and fiction. A ten percent discount is offered on the "flavor" of the month, an ever-changing special topic. Audition information and performer job opportunities are available to clients. They hold author autographing sessions and publish a newsletter with information about the store.

The coffeehouse section of the store offers coffee, drinks, soups, sandwiches, and deserts. Best of all is the discussion you may find among patrons.

The store is wheelchair accessible and stays open past the traditional bookstore times.

School of Metaphysics Bookstore

Metaphysics

6818 N. Ashland
Chicago, IL 60626
312-784-5377
Hours: Appointment only

Season To Taste Books Ltd.

Cooking

911 W. School St.
Chicago, IL 60657
312-327-0210
Hours: Mon.-Fri. 10-7;
Sat. 10-6; Sun. noon-6

If you're planning a special meal, don't go to the grocery store first. Go to Season to Taste Books Ltd. where you can choose a cookbook from the 10,000 titles in stock. If you choose a recipe you don't quite understand, don't skip it and forge ahead. Talk with Barry Bluestein and Kevin Morrissey at Season to Taste Books. They're happy help you with questions.

If you're like me and haven't a clue as to where to start, Barry and Kevin will help you find the cookbook to match your skills. They have both written cookbooks and their culinary expertise is beyond measure. Also in stock is a small section of rare cookbooks. They will happily search for a cookbook to meet your needs.

Unfortunately, the store is not wheelchair accessible.

Selected Works Bookstore

Scholarly

3510 N. Broadway
Chicago, IL 60613
312-975-0002
Hours: Daily noon-9

Established in 1984, Selected Works Bookstore continues to stock books to please the scholarly reader. Over 15,000 titles cover humanities, philosophy, theology, literature, occult and music. Some used music sheets are available.

Because Selected Works is located in a basement, it is not wheelchair accessible.

Spanish Speaking Book Store

Gen. Spanish   5127 N. Clark
                                          Chicago, IL 60640
                                          312-878-2117
                                          <u>Hours:</u> Mon.-Sat. 10:30-6:30

Habla espanole? If you do, you'll find a Spanish bookstore
appropriately named Spanish Speaking Book Store at 5127 N. Clark.
With classical and Spanish music playing, patrons browse the 4,500 titles
concerning fine arts, fiction, children's books, humor and more. Music
cassettes and compact discs are available.

Special orders are welcome and the store manager, Tomas G.
Bissonnette, is available for consultation regarding educational programs
and curriculums.

The store is wheelchair accessible and mass transit is nearby.

The Stars Our Destination

Science fiction   2942 N. Clark
                                          Chicago, IL 60657
                                          312-871-2722
                                          <u>Hours:</u> Mon.-Sat. 11-9;
                                          Sun. 12-6

When you want to blast off to another world, aim your spaceship at
The Stars Our Destination on North Clark Street. You'll land in the
middle of a terrific collection of books from another galaxy.

"We do our best to carry every science fiction, fantasy, and horror
novel in print," said Alice Bentley, partner/manager of the store. To
fulfill that quest, The Stars Our Destination stocks small press science
fiction that may not be on the big bookseller's shelves.

After you've made your book selections, check out all the other
items available: special T-shirts, Star Trek models, pins, posters, videos
and music cassette tapes.

"Our staff welcomes questions and conversation," Alice added. The
staff understands their stock and enjoys discussing the literature and
finding the perfect match for your taste. The staff specializes in gossip
mongering on all aspects of the science fiction field.

The Stars Our Destination is customer oriented. They display covers
of up-coming releases, tag Hugo and Nebula nominees, and have a
popular recommended reading section. They publish a newsletter,

sponsor author autographing sessions, conduct readings, and throw parties for sci-fi buffs. Special orders are filled upon request. After purchasing a $2.00 discount card, you can purchase books at 10% off for three months.

There is one small step to get into the store so those who can do wheelies in their wheelchairs can get inside where the store is completely accessible. Mass transit is available. Like anywhere in this part of the city, parking is pure luck.

Explore this brave new world and make the stars your destination.

Stern's Book Service

Psychology
                                       5804 N. Magnolia
Chicago, IL 60660
312-561-2121
<u>Hours:</u> Mon.-Fri. 10-6; Sat. 10-4

"Important and readable books in the fields of psychology, therapy, and human potential," concisely describes Stern's Book Service. With over 4,000 titles for the professional involved with the therapy process and over 1,000 self-help books, Stern's Book Service is indeed a specialist in people.

If you are in charge of setting up a conference, seminar, or workshop for your club or work, you can call Kathryn K. Stern and she will set up a display of books for sale that directly relates to the topics discussed during conferences, seminars, workshops. Perhaps you would like to distribute lists of reference books to all the people attending your workshop. Stern's Book Service will supply you with the lists you need. For example, if you are conducting a seminar about substance abuse, Stern's will complement your seminar by setting up a display of self-help books covering addiction recovery, ACOA, co-dependency, drug abuse, eating disorders, self-esteem, and more. If your seminar is attended by professionals, the display would include books aimed at them including counseling, group therapy, substance abuse, and therapeutic games.

Discounts are available on purchases of ten or more of a single book. The store is not wheelchair accessible but Stern's offers a number of options including mail order and phone order. Shipping is done by UPS ground service. They will ship via next-day and second-day air service upon request. Foreign shipments are no problem. If you do visit the store, parking is available behind the store.

Call Stern's Book Service for more details about their special display service. They can make your seminar special.

Transitions Bookplace

Spiritual

1015 W. Armitage
Chicago, IL 60614
312-348-7777
Hours: Mon.-Sat 10-9; Sun. 11-6

A spiritual bookstore, Transitions Bookplace carries a large inventory of psychology, women's studies, grief, and co-dependency books. The store has a one step entrance, so a wheelchair user may require some assistance. An employee described Transitions Bookplace as comparable to a Los Angeles bookstore, so homesick Californians may especially enjoy Transitions.

Unabridged Books Inc.

Gay & Lesbian

3251 N. Broadway
Chicago, IL 60657
312-883-9119
Hours: Mon.-Fri. 10-10;
Sat.& Sun. 10-8

Have you stood in front of a group of books, knowing you want one of them, but not sure which one you really should buy? Unabridged Books helps you out by placing yellow shelf signs under staff recommended titles.

"All six of our staff members enjoy books and share our enthusiasm about our favorites with patrons," said Ed Devereux, owner/manager of Unabridged Books Inc.

With 20,000 titles specializing in gay issues, women's studies, and fiction, the store has an excellent selection of sale books. Special orders are welcome.

In addition to selling books, magazines, and calendars, Unabridged Books distributes free community newspapers such as the Reader. A community bulletin board is near the front of the store. They also sell tickets for events sponsored by non-profit groups.

Music ranging from classical to new age plays throughout the store. Unabridged Books Inc. distributes its own newsletter and sponsors special author autographing sessions.

The store is wheelchair accessible from outside and within. Mass transit is nearby and parking is available on the street.

Waldenbooks

General

616 W. Diversey Pkwy.
Chicago, IL 60614
312-549-3792
Hours: Mon.-Fri. 10-9;
Sat. 10-7; Sun. 11-6

The White Elephant Shop

Used-Fairs

2380 N. Lincoln Ave.
Chicago, IL 60614
312-281-3747
Hours: Thurs. 10:30-6;
Mon.-Wed., Fri., Sat. 10-5;
Sun. 10-5

"All of the proceeds from this shop go directly to Children's Memorial Hospital," said Sonni Hill, Director of the White Elephant Shop.

The store has kept this tradition since it was founded in 1916. Today, volunteers manage a terrific store that is open everyday. The exciting news for book lover's is their book sales. They coordinate six book sales every year; three sales for hardcover books and three sales for paperbacks. At the hardcover sale, they offer six to eight thousand titles and at the paperback sale, they often have ten to twelve thousand titles. Topics cover a wide range of interests since the books are all donated. Call the shop to find out the dates of the sales.

In the store they sell books at full price for the first two days they are in stock and then begin reducing the price. Volume fluctuates depending upon donations.

The store is wheelchair accessible and mass transit is close by. If you're travelling by car, you can park in the hospital parking lot.

Be sure to attend their giant book fairs. You can find books to purchase for your own library, perhaps donate a few old titles, and benefit children.

Women & Children First, Inc.

Women & Child

5233 N. Clark
Chicago, IL 60614
312-769-9299
Hours: Mon. & Tues. 11-7;
Wed.-Fri. 11-9; Sat. 10-7;
Sun. 11-6

The name of the store lets you know just what will be found inside. This popular store recently moved to this location while maintaining the quality of the books they stock. Clients will certainly follow them to this new address.

For women, the books include titles in feminism, health, fiction, careers, poetry, biography, newspapers and stationery. Children can stay in a special play area while Mom browses the books. Children's books emphasize the importance of women's roles more than most first grade readers. Books also include multi-cultural interests.

Women and Children First Bookstore is wheelchair accessible. Some corners and aisles in the store are a bit tight.

Yesterday

Used

1143 W. Addison St.
Chicago, IL 60613
312-248-8087
Hours: Mon.-Sat. 1-7; Sun. 2-6

It seems like only yesterday when you tossed those old Life magazines out of the garage. And it seems like yesterday that you were trading 8 x 10 photographs of your favorite movie stars or swapping baseball cards with your best buddy. Yesterday is today at Yesterday. What? Yesterday is the name of a store on West Addison in Chicago that sells books, magazines, records, toys, figurines, lobby cards, comics, and anything else you remember from your past.

The book selection covers biographies, games, romances, fiction, sports, performing arts, cinema, film, theatre, and science fiction. Thousands of magazines and newspapers are available. Owner Tom Boyle says that he has the largest collection of Life magazines in the midwest. In addition to hundreds of books in stock, Yesterday sells toys, games and figurines.

"We are primarily a popular culture store," explained Tom.

Yesterday has two steps to get inside but is wheelchair accessible within the store. Off-street parking is available and, like most everywhere in Chicago, mass transit is available.

Chicago Northwest

A & A Prosser Booksellers

Religious, Used

3118 N. Keating Ave.
Chicago, IL 60641
312-685-7680
Hours: Mail Order Only

For over thirty-five years Andrew Prosser has been tracking down some of the most beautiful and treasured books in existence. He operates his business by mail or telephone and by appointment only. His collection has over 15,000 titles stored in attractive glass enclosed book cases.

He specializes in out-of-print pre-Vatican II Catholic authors. Included in his antiquarian collection are books discussing literature, fiction, cinema, biography, mystery, romance and sports.

Call A & A Prosser for an experienced used book dealer to find that special book you want for your library.

Alverno Religious Art & Books

Religious

5245-53 W. Irving Park Road
Chicago, IL 60641
312-286-5353
Hours: Mon. & Thurs. 9:30-9;
Tues., Wed., Fri., Sat. 9:30-6

"In over 32 years we have earned the reputation of not disappointing a customer," said Anne Prete, President of Alverno Religious Art & Books.

You certainly will be pleased with the service when you visit their store. They will work to help authors and educators find the resource materials they need. They also offer workshops, author autographing sessions and publish a newsletter to keep customers informed. As a special, unique service, Mary, the owner's daughter and professional musician, will be happy to assist choir directors and musicians select music and liturgy.

In the store you can browse through the 20,000 titles in the departments of religion, theatre, education, biography, and black studies. Also for sale are a selection of music cassette tapes, videos, and church goods.

The store is wheelchair accessible. Alverno Religious Art & Books was established in 1959.

American Indian Books

American Indian, Text

2838 W. Peterson
Chicago, IL 60659
312-761-5000
Hours: Mon.-Thurs. 12-7

Since 1980 Chicagoland book lovers have enjoyed browsing at a unique bookstore that also is mobile. The permanent location of American Indian Books is also the location of NAES College. In addition, the store operates a mobile bookstore that travels to pow-wows, neighborhood festivals, and community events.

As their name implies, American Indian Books sells exclusively Native American topics including history, cookery, reference, environment, archaeology, arts and crafts, education, games, literature, women's studies, and children's books. They also have audio books available.

All of the books are reviewed by college staff members and tribe members to ensure the accuracy of the material. Books used by NAES College Bookstore are found in the bookstore. There are between 500-650 titles. The bookstore is the source for NAES College information.

The bookstore is mainly staffed by volunteers and is wheelchair accessible. When you are looking for something new to read, check the selections available at American Indian Books.

American Management Assoc. Bookstore

Business Management

8655 W. Higgins Rd.
Chicago, IL 60631
312-693-5511
Hours: Mon.-Fri. 8-5; closed for lunch between 11:30-12:30

You don't have to be a member of the American Management Association to shop in their bookstore located near the Marriot off the Cumberland exit of I-90. But if you are a member, you'll receive a ten percent discount.

A good selection of approximately 3,000 titles are in stock. Topics include business, management, engineering, accounting, and computers from all publishers, not just the AMA. Special orders are given special attention and usually ordered the same day they receive the request. The store does ship books all over the world.

In addition to books they carry at-home study courses, videos, audio-cassettes, and some foreign language tapes and books for the business-man. In-house training programs are offered.

There is a two inch step to enter the building and if wheelchairs don't want to jump the curb, a mail and telephone service are available. The store was established in 1975.

If you work in the business world, you'll find solutions to your questions in many of the books stocked. Be sure to stop by.

Arcade Bookshop

Religious

7238 W. Foster Ave.
Chicago, IL 60656
312-631-4440
Hours: Sat. only 10-4

The Book Market

Magazines

4018 N. Cicero
Chicago, IL 60641
312-545-7377
Hours: Mon.-Fri. 10-9;
Sat. 10-6; Sun. 12-5

Imagine the most remote, obscure topic, say trading your airplane. Then design a magazine written specifically about that topic. Chances are, the magazine is already being published. If so, you'll find it at The Book Market which carries just about every magazine available for newsstand sales. What about that trading your airplane idea? Already done. It's called "Trade-a-Plane."

Not obscure enough for you? How about "Tombstone Epitaph" which is a history of the town of Tombstone, Arizona. This magazine's popularity is growing, according to Dave who knows every magazine in the store.

You'll find "Hemming's Motor News," specialty magazines for almost every car made, and "Owner/Operator" for professional truck drivers. For your child, there is "Racing for Kids" which contains news about go-kart and various other racing sports for children.

When you think of the entertainment field, you're sure to think of "Variety." The Book Market is stocked with other more off-the-wall entertainment magazines such as "Venice" and "Paper." For environmental issues, pick up "Garbage" magazine. You have heard of Japanese business management. Now you can bring the Japanese flavor into your home with the magazine, "Mangajin." It covers stories about Japanese animation and comics and also how to teach yourself the Japanese language.

Perhaps literary magazines interest you. The Book Market stocks a tremendous range of literary magazines such as "Green Mountain Review," "Long Shot," and reviews from many university presses including Ontario Review, and Indiana Review. Don't forget such classic magazines as "Black Ice," "White Walls," and the infamous "Boing Boing".

Overwhelmed yet? Maybe you should buy "Fact Sheet 5". This is a magazine published in index form that lists what other magazines are writing about.

You'll find foreign, political, history, and crafts magazines in addition to domestic and foreign newspapers. Most of the foreign newspapers are British but they also sell Spanish and French newspapers.

Of course, a store named The Book Market must sell books. Most are general interest, mass market books but they have an incredible selection of books about the American West. Other bookstores in Chicago even recommend that clients visit the Book Market to find virtually every Western book in print. If you're looking for a specific book not in stock, you can use The Book Market's computer to delve into "Books in Print" which lists over one million books and 35,000 publishers.

Physically, the store is wheelchair accessible, off-street parking is available and mass transit is close. Senior citizens receive special discounts. Many books are available for a 10% reduction from the cover price.

As you can guess, employees are well-informed and very organized people. With a massive stock that changes weekly, they have developed a coding system with colored stickers so they can tell the date a magazine entered the store and who published the magazine.

If, by some wild chance, the Book Market doesn't have the magazine you're looking for, tell them as much information about the magazine as you can. They can track the magazine down and get hold of it just for you.

Owner Joe Angelostri isn't kidding when he says, "We have the largest magazine selection in Chicago." You'll be amazed. The Book Market is a fun place to experience.

Chicago Bibles & Books

Religious   3931 W. Irving Park Rd.
                                             Chicago, IL 60618
                                             312-478-0550
                                             Hours: Mon.-Sat. 10-6

"Our goal is to get God's word out into people's hands so they can know His riches and eternal plan," says Barbara Azzarello, Manager of Chicago Bibles & Books.

Over 25,000 titles adorn their shelves in all areas of Christian literature. Special departments include children's books, Bible study reference books, theology, Spanish language bibles, Greek and Hebrew selections, and large type books. As a special treat for their customers, they sponsor personal bible studies.

The store has one step to enter but is wheelchair accessible within. Quantity discounts are available for those purchasing more than fifty dollars.

Chicago Hebrew Bookstore

Religious, Hebrew   2942 W. Devon Ave.
                                             Chicago, IL 60659
                                             312-973-6636
                                             Hours: Mon.-Wed. 9-6;
                                             Thurs. 9-7; Fri. 9-4
                                             (in winter, Fri. 9-2)

"We try to make our customers comfortable," said David Gross, manager of the Chicago Hebrew Bookstore. "We supply information without pressuring customers."

The store carries a complete line of Judaic literature, menorahs, candlesticks, candles, knives, and more. Books are available in English, Hebrew and Yiddish. Additional services include imprinting, engraving, gift wrapping and UPS delivery.

Jewish and classical music soothes the customers while they browse. Off-street parking and mass transit are available. Although the store has no stairs to impede wheelchairs, it is tight and unmanageable for wheelchairs in the aisles.

Established in 1979, they now stock well over 2,000 titles.

Covenant Bookstore

Religious, Text

3200 W. Foster Ave.
Chicago, IL 60625
312-478-4676
Hours: Mon.-Fri. 9-5; Sat. 10-5

Covenant Bookstore stocks Christian books, church supplies, North Park College textbooks, school supplies, and insignia clothing. The store is wheelchair accessible.

Crown Books

General

4842 W. Irving Park Rd.
Chicago, IL 60641
312-736-0886
Hours: Mon.-Fri. 9-8;
Sat. 10-6; Sun. 11-5

DeVry Bookstore

Text, Electronics

3300 N. Campbell Ave.
Chicago, IL 60618
312-929-8500
Hours: Mon. 9-12 & 1-3;
Tues.-Thurs. 9-12, 1-3,
& 5:30-7:30

Open to both the public and students, the DeVry Institute of Technology Bookstore stocks technical books about electronics, computers, accounting, and business. Other items for sale are calculators, tape recorders, oscilloscopes, electronic templates, mechanical drafting paper and assorted supplies.

Located inside the institute, the bookstore is wheelchair accessible. There are two locations of the school and bookstore; the other is in west suburban Lombard.

The Emperor's Headquarters

Militaria

5744 W. Irving Park
Chicago, IL 60634
312-777-7307
Hours: Mon.-Wed. 12-8;
Thurs-Sat. 10-12 pm; Sun. 1-10

With lively military music playing, patrons select books and magazines relating to militaria (including history and biographies) at The Emperor's Headquarters in Chicago.

Two thousand titles are lined up in an orderly manner on the shelves in this shop that also offers military miniatures and prints. The Emperor's Headquarters also sponsors author autographing and craft demonstrations. Special book orders are welcome.

Parking and mass transit are available. However, the store does have eight steps to enter which makes it difficult for strollers and impossible for wheelchairs. Once inside the store, it is wheelchair accessible and restrooms are available. No seating is available within the store.

Everybody's Bookstore

Used

2120 W. Devon Ave.
Chicago, IL 60659
312-764-0929
Hours: Mon.-Sat. 12-6;
Thurs. 2-6

With 10,000 fiction and non-fiction used books, Everybody's Bookstore also carries many comic books and old magazines. The business was established in 1979. Although wheelchairs can enter the store, the aisles are narrow and at times difficult to maneuver around.

Ezra A. Cook Bookstore

Masonic

6604 W. Irving Park Rd.
Chicago, IL 60634
312-685-1101
Hours: Mon.-Fri. 9-1pm and
3-4:30pm

Specializing in Masonic and Eastern-star literature, the Ezra A. Cook Bookstore was established in 1900. The new and used books total 165 titles. Customers are members of the many Masonic lodges in the

Chicago-area and around the world. The bookstore serves both walk-in and mail order customers.

A 25% discount is available if twelve or more copies of the same book are ordered. The store is wheelchair accessible from the outside but not accessible inside.

Gerald J. Cielec Books

Religious

2248 N. Kedvale Ave.
Chicago, IL 60639
312-235-2326
Hours: Mail order only

Since the establishment of his business in 1979, Gerald J. Cielec has conducted his bookselling business by mail order only. He deals in used books specializing in fine art, performing art, architecture, photography, arts and crafts. He has approximately 2,000 books in stock. He does special order books for patrons.

Impact Book Store

Religious

3917 W. North
Chicago, IL 60647
312-252-4992
Hours: Mon.-Sat. 10-5

In addition to over 2,000 titles, Impact Bookstore sells video and music cassette tapes. The focus of the books is religious with many books written in Spanish. Established in 1974, the store is wheelchair accessible.

J.F. Morrow & Sons

Religious

6015 N. Milwaukee Ave.
Chicago, IL 60646
312-631-8844
Hours: Mon.-Fri. 9-5:30; Sat. 9-4
(summer Sat. 9-noon)

Since the store was established in 1955, J.F. Morrow & Sons has carried a fine reputation of religious books, church supplies, alter bread, candles, and other religious items. They stock 1,000 titles with most focusing on Catholicism.

J.F. Morrow & Sons sells both wholesale and retail. The store is wheelchair accessible. During the summer the store closes at noon on Saturdays.

Kazi Publications Inc.

Arabic/Religious   3023 W. Belmont Ave.
                                            Chicago, IL 60618
                                            312-267-7001
                                            <u>Hours:</u> Mon.-Sat. 11-5:30

When you step into Kazi Publications, you step into an Arabic oasis filled with your favorite things: books. According to Liaquat Ali, manager, it is the largest Islamic-Middle East book and supply store in North America.

While Arabic music plays, you can browse the cases filled with 3,000 different titles written in Arabic, English, Urdu, and Farsi languages. If you can't find what you're looking for on the shelves, they will special order books for you from all over the world. In addition, Kazi Publications stocks all Islamic and Middle East supplies.

Some books are discounted at 30-50% off and teachers, schools, and universities are given special discounts. Kazi Publications is totally wheelchair accessible and has off-street parking available. Mass transit is nearby. The store was established in 1972.

Libreria Yuquiyu

Spanish   2546 W. Division
                                            Chicago, IL 60622
                                            312-486-1882
                                            <u>Hours:</u> Mon.-Sat. 9-6

Ninety-five percent of the books you'll find at Libreria Yuquiyu are written in Spanish. More than 1,000 titles include bestsellers, short stories, learning to speak Spanish, and textbooks. The textbooks are used in the lower grades of Chicago public schools. They also have some books especially written for pre-schoolers.

In addition to the business operating by phone and mail order, there is a store that is open everyday except Sunday. The store is wheelchair accessible. Libreria Yuquiyu was established twelve years ago.

Magic Inc.

Magic
5082 N. Lincoln Ave.
Chicago, IL 60625
312-334-2855
Hours: Mon.-Sat. 10:30-5:30 &
mail order

It's no magic trick that has kept Magic Inc. in business for sixty-one years. It's due to the quality of the merchandise available for amateur and experienced magicians.

In addition to over 1,500 books about magic, they stock the supplies necessary for success. Juggling books and tools are also available. The business is open six days per week and also conducts business by phone and mail order. The store is wheelchair accessible.

Metro Golden Memories

Cinema
5425 W. Addison
Chicago, IL 60641
312-965-7763
Hours: Mon.-Sat. 10-6;
Sun. 12-5

"You should stop in to see our store," owner Chuck Schaden of Metro Golden Memories Bookstore invites. "You'll be amazed! We have what we believe is the largest, most complete collection of books on the movies, including film studies, in the mid-west."

With film soundtracks playing as background music, the film-loving patrons not only shop for new and used books but they can rent or buy classic movies and television programs on video tape. They also specialize in old time radio shows available on cassettes and records.

In addition to stocking 3,500 book volumes, you can complement your passion for old movies by purchasing movie T-shirts, coffee mugs, posters, collectors' plates and even replicas of the Maltese Falcon statue and the RCA dog. If that isn't enough for you, you can buy your own Oscar look-alike.

Open seven days per week, Metro Golden Memories is completely wheelchair accessible. Non-metered street parking is available as well as mass transit. Special orders are welcome.

N. Fagin Books

Antiquarian

1039 W. Grand Ave.
Chicago, IL 60622
312-829-5252
<u>Hours:</u> Mon.-Fri. 10-5; Sat. 10-3

"The more technical the better," says Nancy Fagin who searches for books that customers request.

In addition to sniffing out obscure books, Nancy has a store filled with 50,000 books focusing on the arts, anthropology, archeology, zoology, botany, environmental issues, social sciences, science, and Spanish. Discounts are available to dealers.

While you shop, classical music or National Public Radio plays throughout the store. Along with the large book selection, Nancy sells decorative prints for your home and unique native crafts.

There is one step to get into the store which makes it difficult for wheelchairs. Once inside, it is accessible.

National Christian Books-Gifts Dist. Inc.

Religious

4748 N. Pulaski
Chicago, IL 60630
312-777-0099
<u>Hours:</u> Mon.-Sat. 10:30-7

This small store carries 150-200 Christian books and Bibles, gifts, and groceries. Health foods can be ordered and arrive the next day. Established in 1989, the store is wheelchair accessible.

Officer Bob's Paperbacks

Used

4340 N. Milwaukee
Chicago, IL 60641
312-736-9522
<u>Hours:</u> Tues.-Sat. 11-5

If your home has been infested with paperback books, you may want to consider trading them in for others. At Officer Bob's Paperbacks you can do just that for real bargain prices. Over 10,000 books in stock are normally 50 percent off retail prices. If you bring books to exchange, you'll receive an extra 20 percent off.

Books stocked include fiction, children's books, cookery, mystery, romance, health-nutrition, science fiction, sports, arts and crafts, biographies, and even magic and the occult. The shelves are filled with over 10,000 selections.

Owner Ann Samson says patrons can find out-of-print books among her selections including some rare and very old books. Officer Bob's Paperbacks was established in 1981.

Polonia Book Store

Polish

2886 N. Milwaukee
Chicago, IL 60618
312-489-2554
Hours: Mon., Thurs. 10-7;
Tues., Wed., Fri. 10-6;
Sat. 9:30-5:30, mail order

Chicago is known for it's large Polish ethnic population and this Polish bookstore is the largest in the United States. They offer a wide selection of books written in Polish including fiction, poetry, history, religion, reference, cookbooks, magazines, and children's books. They also carry a large selection of books written in English about Polish topics. Polonia Book Store also carries Polish greeting cards, music cassettes, compact discs, posters, and paintings.

They publish an impressive catalogue three times per year which currently reaches 15,000 clients. The store itself has about 3,000 different titles in their stock of 40,000 books. The store is wheelchair accessible, mass transit is close, and parking is on the street.

The store sponsors author autographing sessions and offers discounts to schools, public and university libraries. The staff will special order books.

Specialty stores have a design and flavor all their own. Polonia Book Store is one of the shining stars of foreign book stores. If you don't live close enough to visit, call for a catalogue--you'll be dazzled.

Powner's

Masonic

6604 Irving Park Road
Chicago, IL 60634
312-685-1101

Powner's is associated with the Ezra Cook Bookstore (see description earlier in this chapter).

Rainbow Island Books (Hidden Meanings)

General

4046 N. Milwaukee
Chicago, IL 60641
312-794-1334
Hours: Mon.-Fri. 1pm-8pm;
Sat. & Sun. noon-6 (Call
ahead-may be open longer)

Formerly known as Hidden Meanings Bookstore, Rainbow Island Books stocks from 12-15,000 general interest books. In addition to their terrific selection of books, they also have assorted record albums and magazines.

The bookstore is wheelchair accessible except when aisles become crowded with books stacked on the floor. The store was established in May, 1987.

Rosenblum's World of Judaica, Inc.

Religious

2906 W. Devon Ave.
Chicago, IL 60659
312-262-1700
Hours: Mon. Tues., Wed. 9-6;
Thurs. 9-7; Fri. 9-4; Sun. 10-4

In addition to being Chicago's oldest and largest distributor of Jewish books, Rosenblum's World of Judaica has hundreds of customers outside the Chicago area.

However, Avrom B. Fox, President, says, "Philosophically we serve the city of Chicago and not specific religious denominations. We cater to everyone, Jews and non-Jews."

The store has approximately 10,000 titles on its shelves. They custom order religious articles for weddings and bar/bat mitzots. In addition to keeping books in stock, they sell artwork, ketubot, Jewish sheet music, video's, compact disc's, cassettes, candy, toys, Israeli newspapers, and an assortment of religious articles.

The store is wheelchair accessible. Employees are always happy to assist customers in selecting books on any part of Judaism.

Waldenbooks

General

6465 W. Diversey
Chicago, IL 60635
312-745-8660
<u>Hours:</u> Mon.-Fri. 10-9;
Sat. 10-7; Sun. 10-6

Chicago South

57th Street Books

Scholarly

1301 East 57th St.
Chicago, IL 60637
312-684-1300
Hours: Mon.-Thurs. 10-10;
Fri.-Sat. 10-11pm; Sun. 10-8

A branch of the Seminary Cooperative Bookstore, 57th Street Books stocks a terrific selection of over 50,000 new books. The main focus is scholarly books since the University of Chicago is just down the street.

Because they are in a basement with low ceilings and an uneven cement floor, 57th Street Books quickly becomes a cozy little spot that you can enjoy for hours. With 4,000 square feet, 57th Street Books is attractively designed for the browser to disappear in it's nooks and crannies and twists and turns. An inviting coffee pot of hot brew entices the browser to sit and scan the book review sections of a variety of newspapers.

Special events occur at 57th Street Books on a regular basis. Monthly they conduct a poetry reading series. Children's story-time is held every other week for those younger book lovers aged 3-6.

Unfortunately, the store is not wheelchair accessible. The entrance has three stony steps to descend. For those who can tackle the steps and those able-bodies that don't give it a second thought, be sure to visit this bookstore.

Adventures in Reading

Children's

1525 East 53rd St., Ste. 901
Chicago, IL 60615
312-684-7323
Hours: Mon.-Fri. 1-5; Sat. 11-4

Your pre-schooler and teenager will enjoy reading when they browse through Adventures in Reading. Many of their books are found in local grade schools. If your child can't get enough of reading, you'll be able to buy sets of books similar to ones they see in the classroom. Many of the books present African-American topics oriented toward children.

The store is wheelchair accessible.

African American Book Center

Black Studies   7524 S. Cottage Grove
                                                  Chicago, IL 60619
                                                  312-651-0700
                                                  Hours: Mon.-Fri. 10-6; Sat. 10-5

The African-American Book Center is a place for the whole family. Over 5,000 titles in stock means everyone in the family can find something of interest to read. Topics focus on the African-American experience and include history, political science, music, literature, children's books and family studies. In addition, they sell games, greeting cards, T-shirts, and hats.

They publish a newsletter to keep patrons informed of the many activities the book center sponsors. They throw book parties almost every week and have author autographing sessions.

The African-American Book Center now has three branches. In addition to their main store on Cottage Grove, they are also located at 1807 East 71st Street in Chicago and 3420 W. 183rd Street in Hazelwood.

African American Book Center

Black Studies   1807 East 71st Street
                                                  Chicago, IL 60649
                                                  312-752-2275
                                                  Hours: Mon.-Fri. 11-8; Sat. 11-7

Make a visit to the African-American Book Center and bring the whole family. With over 5,000 titles in stock, everyone in the family will find something of interest to read. Topics focus on the African-American experience and include history, political science, music, literature, children's books and family studies. In addition, they sell games, greeting cards, T-shirts, and hats. They publish a monthly newsletter to keep patrons informed of the many activities the book center sponsors.

African American Book Center

Black Studies

3420 West 183rd Street
Hazelwood, IL 60421
708-798-7995
Hours: Mon.-Sat. 11-8;
Sun. noon-5

The African-American Book Center is a great place to take the entire family. With shelves stocking over 5,000 titles, everyone in the family can choose a book of interest to them. Topics focus on the African-American experience and include history, political science, music, literature, children's books and family studies. In addition, they sell games, greeting cards, T-shirts, and hats. A monthly newsletter is published to publicize the many activities the book center sponsors.

Anne W. Leonard Books

General

1935 W. 95th St.
Chicago, IL 60643
312-239-7768
Hours: Mon.-Fri. 10-6;
Sat. 10-4; Sun. 10-3

Anne W. Leonard has a used bookstore located on 95th Street where she stocks approximately 16,000 hard-cover and paperback books covering subjects such as mystery, literature, sports, black studies, and children's books.

"We carry a general and rather eclectic stock," says Anne. She adds that neighborhood authors stop by to conduct autographing sessions.

The 960 square foot store is wheelchair accessible although the aisles aren't always clear. Anne is always happy to assist anyone in the store.

Chinatown Book and Gifts

Chinese

2214 S. Wentworth
Chicago, IL 60616
312-326-1761
Hours: Daily 9:30am-10pm

At Chinatown Book and Gifts, you'll find approximately 500 books and magazines, most of which are written in Chinese. Other items for sale include wind chimes, umbrellas, mah jong games, and T shirts.

The store is wheelchair accessible and is open seven days per week.

Ex Libris Theological Books

Used Scholarly

1340 E. 55th St.
Chicago, IL 60615
312-955-3456
Hours: Mon.-Sat. noon-6

Located two blocks from the Quad of the University of Chicago in Hyde Park, Ex Libris Theological Books sells used and out-of-print scholarly and theology books, along with some special selections from the 17th century. There are also many books about church history, biblical studies, and the philosophy of religion. The store is wheelchair accessible.

Family Health Education Service

Health

8517 S. State
Chicago, IL 60619
312-488-0229
Hours: Mon.-Thurs. 8-5:30;
Fri. 8-12:30; mail order

A mail order business, Family Health Education Service wants to help you develop a happy and healthy family. Over 500 titles help you in the areas of children, marriage, drug free families, black heritage, and health related books and magazines. They also sell ten different Bibles. Many of the books are printed in large type, others are written in Spanish and French.

A health food store nearby highlights the items you read about. The Family Health Education Service store is wheelchair accessible.

IL Institute of Technology Bookshop

Text

3200 S. Wabash Ave.
Chicago, IL 60616
312-567-3120
Hours: Mon.-Thurs. 8:30-6:30;
Fri. 8:30-5

Although the Illinois Institute of Technology Bookshop is primarily for the Institute's students, it is open to the public. In addition to selling text books and books about architecture, computers, and technology, they sell the needed instruments and office supplies.

The store is wheelchair accessible.

Louis Kiernan, Bookseller

Antiquarian
1342 E. 55th St.
Chicago, IL 60615
312-752-2555
Hours: Mon.-Fri. noon-8:30;
Sat. & Sun. noon-6

Located near the University of Chicago, Louis Kiernan deals in quality used books with a strong emphasis on scholarly books about history, architecture, fine art, literature, philosophy, music, theology, photography and folklore.

Proud of his location in Hyde Park, Louis says that there is no better concentration of quality new and used book stores in the Midwest. Hyde Park also sponsors Chicago's only children's book fair each fall.

Over 30,000 books adorn the shelves and Louis is always willing to purchase books as well as sell them. He will also make house calls in the Chicago area for larger collections.

The store is wheelchair accessible. In tribute to his heritage, Louis sponsors a live traditional Irish band once per year.

According to Louis, "We have the prettiest bookshop cat in Chicago." Is this a challenge to other bookshops?

Modern Bookstore

Labor
3118 S. Halsted
Chicago, IL 60617
312-225-7911
Hours: Tues. & Thurs. 10-6;
Fri. & Sat. 10-7; Sun. noon-5

Modern Bookstore is the descendant of a bookstore that was established over sixty years ago and has occupied locations on Dearborn, in New Town, and Blue Island. The 5,000 books in stock emphasize a labor oriented theme. Included are histories of the Labor Union, social thought, African-American culture and literature, and multi-cultural children's books.

Quarterly they publish a newsletter. Special orders are no problem and the store occasionally sponsors author autographing sessions. The store is wheelchair accessible.

O'Gara & Wilson Booksellers, Ltd.

Antiquarian, ABAA

1311 East 57th Street
Chicago, IL 60637
312-363-0993
Hours: Mon.-Sat. 9am-10pm;
Sun. noon-10

Founded in 1882, O'Gara and Wilson Booksellers is the oldest book store in Chicago. They have long been a Chicago institution held in high esteem by Midwest book lovers. Today they have over 200,000 titles in stock which range from 16th century Latin texts to modern books. Located near the University of Chicago, their stock is scholarly in nature.

O'Gara & Wilson Booksellers are members of the Antiquarian Booksellers Association of America. They operate a branch store in Chesterton, Indiana. The store here has one step to enter, making it difficult for some in wheelchairs.

Topics they have a particular interest in are history, military history, literature, religion, music, archaeology, antiques, and cookery. All eight employees hold Master of Arts degrees which gives them a wealth of knowledge available to you. All you have to do is just ask a question.

Olive-Harvey College (C&W Books Ltd.)

Text

1001 S. Woodlawn
Chicago, IL 60653
312-821-5963
Hours: Call to confirm hours

One of the four locations of C & W Books, this location serves to Olive-Harvey College and the public. Books in stock are textbooks, reference, general interest, and fiction; other items are greeting cards, T-shirts, and miscellaneous supplies.

Due to changing hours that reflect the needs of the school year, call before visiting this bookstore.

Powell's Bookstore

Academic Used

1501 E. 57th Street
Chicago, IL 60637
312-955-7780
Hours: Daily 9am-11pm

A famous book spot in Hyde Park, Powell's Bookstore stocks

between 90-100,000 different used books, many of which are publisher surpluses and not yet used. The store is neatly organized with large signs identifying the categories of books. In the same neighborhood as the University of Chicago, the focus of this branch is mostly academic and general interest. In the basement are science fiction and mystery books. While it is possible for a wheelchair to enter the store, the numerous boxes in the aisles make it extremely difficult for a wheelchair to navigate.

Powell's Bookstore has two other branches: 2850 N. Lincoln and their warehouse and small retail store at 828 S. Wabash.

Powell's Bookstore

Used

828 S. Wabash
Chicago, IL 60619
312-341-0748
Hours: Mon.-Fri. 10:30-8:30;
Sat. 10-10; Sun. noon-8

This branch of Powell's Bookstore houses their main warehouse and a small retail store. They stock over 100,000 used books. It is not wheelchair accessible.

Richard Adamiak

Antiquarian

1700 E. 56th St. No. 3604
Chicago, IL 60637
312-955-4571
Hours: Appointment and mail order only

An antiquarian selling used and rare books, Richard Adamiak sells books by mail order and appointment only. His 5,000 titles are about economics, law, history, and literature. Many have fine collector-quality bindings. His business was established in 1971.

Scholars' Books, Inc.

General
1379 E. 53rd Street
Chicago, IL 60615
312-288-6565
Hours: Mon.-Thurs. 11-7;
Fri. & Sat. 11-8; Sun. 12-5

Scholars' Books rewards their patrons with discounts directly based upon your yearly purchases. Once your purchases total $50, you'll receive a 10% discount. When you reach $200, you'll get a 15% discount and finally when your total reaches $500, you'll get a 20% discount.

Another unique offering at Scholars' Books is their sale and repair of computers, sale of gifts, and rental of videos. But don't forget their main interest: books. They have approximately 10,000 volumes in stock, many in Chinese and Japanese, most new, some used. Special topics they carry include martial arts, oriental history, cooking, philosophy, religion, and social sciences.

Non-book items for sale include computers, audio tapes, and a variety of gift items. The store also publishes its own newsletter.

Scholars' Books is wheelchair accessible. Off-street parking and mass transit are nearby.

Seminary Cooperative Bookstore Inc

General
5757 S. University Ave.
Chicago, IL 60637
312-752-1959
Hours: Mon.-Fri. 8:30-9;
Sat. 10-6; Sun. noon-6

Located on the campus of the University of Chicago in Hyde Park, the Seminary Cooperative Bookstore, Inc. stocks over 100,000 new books of general interest and scholarly flavor. Academic books covering every topic can be found on their shelves. Open everyday, the bookstore is "reflective of the neighborhood," according to one employee. The store has 3,000 square feet of enjoyment for the book lover.

The co-op was founded by students of the University of Chicago. Anyone can join the co-op and receive a 10% discount. The bookstore is wheelchair accessible but not easy to maneuver around. There is an elevator in the building. Call ahead for details on the best way for a wheelchair to gain access to the store (which is in the basement).

Chicago South

The Suq-Oriental Institute

History

1155 E. 58th St.
Chicago, IL 60637
312-702-9520
Hours: Tues. 10-4; Sun. 12-4;
Wed. 10-8:30; Thurs.-Sat. 10-4;

Are you looking for that hard-to-find book written in Sumerian? Or is it Egyptian hieroglyph you want? Maybe it's frankincense and myrrh you need to set the mood while you peruse your maps of Mesopotamia, Egypt, and Assyria.

You'll find it all in the little bookstore of the Suq-Oriental Institute. After touring the unique small museum, a bookstore visit is a must. Staffed by volunteers, the bookstore offers a ten percent discount to members on all merchandise which also includes jewelry, T-shirts, and assorted gifts from the Ancient Near East.

The museum is wheelchair accessible via the back door. Discover this tiny museum in Hyde Park. When you find it, you have found a unique treasure in Chicago.

University of Chicago Bookstore

General

970 E. 58th St.
Chicago, IL 60637
312-702-8729
Hours: Mon.-Sat. 9-5

On the first floor of the University of Chicago's Bookstore in Hyde Park, the general public is welcome to browse and purchase books ranging from academic to cartoons. Naturally, you can also find books published by the University of Chicago Press.

The general bookstore stocks over 80,000 titles with subjects featuring literature, computer science, medicine, science, psychology, history, business, economics, reference, foreign languages, travel, humor, and even children's books. They carry a small selection of popular fiction, mystery, and science fiction. They also have a large magazine section.

Also on the first floor is a great little take-out deli. Upstairs is the textbook department which additionally features U. of C. gifts, stationery items, along with photographic services and equipment. There is also a department for office dictating equipment, FAX machines, telephones, and more at competitive prices. Unlike the ground floor, these departments are only open during the week and are not wheelchair accessible.

University of Chicago students, faculty, staff, and alumni receive a 10% discount at the general bookstore. On street parking is available but can be difficult to find, depending upon the college schedule and whether there is snow on the ground (the area is usually poorly plowed). The general bookstore is wheelchair accessible although corners in the 5,600 square foot store are sometimes tight.

Chicago Magazine named the University of Chicago Bookstore as the best university bookstore in town. With more than 80,000 titles, any book lover will delight in spending hours at this bookstore. You'll find titles you didn't know existed and surely won't be disappointed at this store.

World Journal & Bookstore

Chinese   2235 S. Wentworth
                                       Chicago, IL 60616
                                       312-842-8080
                                       Hours: Daily 10-7

With over 10,000 titles located in two different stores in Chicago, World Journal Bookstore stocks Chinese books in computers, cookery, fiction, mystery, psychology, romance, travel and tourism, philosophy, women's studies, economics, health and nutrition, humor, medicine, music photography, science fiction, games and puzzles, children's books, magazines, and foreign newspapers. Periodically, the store sponsors craft demonstrations.

The stores are not wheelchair accessible.

Chicago Southwest

Chicago Law Book Company

Law

4814 S. Pulaski Rd.
Chicago, IL 60632
312-376-1711
Hours: Mon.-Fri. 9-6; Sat. 9-1;
Sunday by appointment

When you travel abroad and tell people that you hale from Chicago, they still can't seem to help pretending they have a tommy gun in hand while stuttering, "Rat-tat-tat-a-tat." Like it or not, Chicago's crime history is infamous. If you want to read more about Chicago's illustrious past, visit the Chicago Law Book Company.

Under the watchful eyes of a limited edition lithograph of Clarence Darrow, you can browse through the 35,000 titles regarding Chicago's crimes, law biographies, American legal history, and all law related books. Patrons include lawyers, law students, paralegals, police officers, and anyone else with an interest in the law.

In addition to books, the Chicago Law Book Company stocks audio and video tapes relating to the law and gifts for lawyers, law students, and paralegals.

"No title is impossible to acquire," is the motto of the store. They search the world for any new or out-of-print books. Recognizing the lawyer's need for information, the Chicago Law Book Company will special order books.

The store is wheelchair accessible and mass transit is close by.

If the names Leopold, Nathan, Darrow, and Gertz have meaning for you, you'll probably want to check out the terrific selection of new, used, and antiquarian books.

Draugus Lithuanian Daily Friend

Lithuania
4545 West 63rd St.
Chicago, IL 60629
312-585-9500
Hours: Mon.-Fri. 8:30-5:30;
Sat. 8:30-noon

In the quest for truth in an evolving world, the Draugus Lithuanian Daily Friend has been publishing the truth about Lithuania for the last 81 years. Published Tuesday through Saturday, the newspaper has been a source of the latest Lithuanian news for all of Chicagoland.

They also write, publish, and sell books written in English and Lithuanian. Many books are used by schools teaching the Lithuanian heritage and some are sent to Lithuania. With a large Lithuanian population in Chicago, we a fortunate to have a self-supporting publisher in our city.

John Rybski Bookseller

Antiquarian
2319 W. 47th Place
Chicago, IL 60609
312-847-5082
Hours: Call for appt.

Kennedy-King College (C&W Books Ltd.)

Text
6800 S. Wentworth
Chicago, IL 60652
312-224-0086
Hours: Call to confirm hours

With textbooks, T-shirts, and assorted books and supplies, this branch of C & W Books serves Kennedy-King College. Like the other three locations, call ahead to confirm hours. The bookstore is wheelchair accessible.

R.J. Daley College (C&W Books Ltd.)

Text

7500 S. Pulaski
Chicago, IL 60652
312-581-3200
<u>Hours:</u> Basically 9-5; call ahead
to confirm

C & W Books has four locations. Each is associated with one of the city's colleges. They each sell textbooks, reference, fiction, and some general interest books. They also have greeting cards, T-shirts, and miscellaneous goods that are appreciated by students. The stores are all basically open from 9am-5pm weekdays but you should call ahead since the hours fluctuate with the school year.

Other locations are listed in the sections of this book.

Saint Xavier College Bookstore

Text

103 St. & Central Park Ave.
Chicago, IL 60655
312-779-3300
<u>Hours:</u> Mon.-Fri. 8-7; Sat. 8-1;
summer hours: 9-4:30

With more than 900 titles in stock, the Saint Xavier College Bookstore sells textbooks, reference, general interest, newspapers, school supplies, sportswear with the school's emblem, and, needed by kids of all ages, candy. Most of the books are new although there are a few used books. The store is especially strong in Nursing books. A few small gifts are available.

The store is wheelchair accessible. Call to confirm the store's hours since it changes to reflect the needs of the changing school year.

V & H Stationery Co. Book Dept.

Text

3908 West 79th
Chicago, IL 60652
312-585-2220
<u>Hours:</u> Vary according to school
year, call ahead

In addition to supplying Daley College students with textbooks and supplies, V & H Stationery Company Book Department is the only bookstore in Chicago that also sells IFFT (firemen training) books and

Civil Service test preparation books. They also sell new and used paperbacks. They have approximately 4,000 titles.

The store is wheelchair accessible. The hours they are open vary according to the college schedule. Call ahead if you plan to stop here.

Waldenbooks

General

Ford City S/Ctr. 7601 S. Cicero
Chicago, IL 60652
312-581-4833
Hours: Mon.-Fri. 10-9;
Sat. 10-6; Sun. 11-5

Chicago West

Community Bible & Book Co., Inc.

Religious

1502 S. St. Louis Ave.
Chicago, IL 60623
312-522-1006
Hours: Mon.-Sat. 11-6

Established in 1963, the Community Bible & Book Company sells Christian books, Bibles, and a variety of church supplies. The front door is narrow which may present a problem for wheelchair accessibility.

Frog Tool Co. Book Dept.

Woodworking

700 W. Jackson
Chicago, IL 60661
312-648-1270
Hours: Mon.-Fri. 9-5; Sat. 9-3

To find everything you've ever wanted to know about woodworking, visit the Frog Tool Company at 700 West Jackson in Chicago. With over 900 titles all about woodworking, you're sure to find just what you need to finish that home repair or project.

"We are the main suppliers of woodworking hand tools in the Midwest," said Richard Watkins, President.

Whether you're a beginning woodworker or a professional carpenter, you'll find high quality materials for the job at the Frog Tool Company. Employees receive special training to answer your questions.

The store is 2,500 square feet large and has five steps to enter. However, the store does offer materials by mail order and is accessible to wheelchairs once inside. Off street parking is not available but mass transit is close.

If wood is your thing, think Frog Tool Company.

Helix Ltd.

Photography

310 S. Racine Ave.
Chicago, IL 60607
312-421-6000
Hours: Mon., Tues., Wed., Fri.
9-5:30; Thurs. 9-7; Sat. 9-5

With the biggest underwater book and photo collection in Chicago, Daisy Rios, buyer with Helix Ltd. is proud of the 1,500 new book selections. Helix carries an outstanding reputation among photographers so you'll be sure to find the best of photography books in this store.

In addition to photo reference books, Helix stocks beautiful fine art, cinema, film, and photography related electronic books. Once you see their underwater photography books, you'll want to dive yourself. All the merchandise and accessories are at your fingertips here.

Seventeen employees are ready for your questions whether you've been a professional photographer for years or the last camera you took a picture with was a Brownie.

There is one step to jump wheelchairs onto but inside the store is accessible. Parking, mass transit, and seating within the store are available.

If you're a camera bug, you'll be sure to enjoy a shutter stop at Helix Ltd.

Logins Medical Center Bookstore

Medical Texts

1910 W. Harrison
Chicago, IL 60612
312-733-4544
Hours: Mon.-Fri. 8:30-5:30;
Sat. 8:30-1

You don't have to be a physician to purchase books at the Logins Medical Center Bookstore. In addition to medical textbooks, they sell many Nursing, Physical Therapy, and Allied Health textbooks.

In stock are 4,000 books and they have speedy access to 15,000 more titles. The store is not wheelchair accessible.

Malcolm X College (C&W Books Ltd.)

Text

1900 W. Van Buren
Chicago, IL 60612
312-829-6482
<u>Hours:</u> Call to confirm times

The bookstore at Malcolm X College supplies the college's students and the public with textbooks, fiction, reference, and general interest books. Call ahead to confirm hours that the store is open.

Marxist-Leninist Books

Revolutionary

1631 W. 18th St.
Chicago, IL 60608
312-243-5302
<u>Hours:</u> Tues. 5pm-7pm;
Sat. noon-6

Established in 1979, Marxist-Leninist Books rings true to their name by stocking works of Marx, Lenin, Engels, and information about the international movement and worker's advocate news. Many books are written in Spanish but most are in English.

The store is not wheelchair accessible.

Rush University Bookstore

Text

600 S. Paulina
Chicago, IL 60612
312-942-5845
<u>Hours:</u> Mon.-Fri. 8:30-5;
call to confirm

In addition to textbooks and reference books used by students of Rush University, this bookstore also sells college insignia clothing, greeting cards, and book bags. The store is wheelchair accessible.

Thomas Joyce and Company

Antiquarian

411 S. Sangamon
Chicago, IL 60607
312-738-1933
Hours: Mon.-Sat. 10-5; call to
confirm hours and address

Thomas Joyce is one of the friendliest booksellers in Chicago. Well, at least he was in Chicago as *The Book Lover's Guide* went to press. The last time I spoke with Tom, he was planning to re-locate his business and dramatically expand his inventory. Therefore, you should call the phone number listed above and the telephone company will give you his new phone number.

Right now, Tom's business has a collection of 7,000 rare books, first editions, vintage law books, out-of-print Americana, medical books, reference books and literature. Tom couldn't disclose his plans for expansion, but I'm sure it will be a terrific endeavor.

Tom does out-of-print book searches and offers book repair advice. His business is a labor of love. In the bookselling business since 1975, Tom is happy to discuss the rare books you may be searching for.

The store on South Sangamon has six steps to enter making it impossible for wheelchairs but his new location may be more accessible.

UIC Health Sciences Store

Science

828 S. Wolcott
Chicago, IL 60612
312-413-5550
Hours: Mon.-Fri. 8-5:30; Sat. 9-5

Students of UIC Health Science Studies and the public are welcome to shop at the bookstore. Located on two levels, the store sells new and used medical textbooks for students studying all areas of health care. The general interest new book section is the only one in the neighborhood. With a large fiction department, the bookstore also sells children's books, and business, computer, and electronics books.

The bookstore carries much more in addition to books: school and office supplies, medical instruments, UIC logo imprinted clothing, and miscellaneous general merchandise. For rent are videos, microscopes, and medical instruments.

The main floor is wheelchair accessible but the lower level is down a flight of stairs. Downstairs are the medical books and medical supplies.

Univ. of IL at Chicago Epi-Center Book Store

Text

750 S. Halsted
Chicago, IL 60607
312-413-5500
Hours: Mon.-Thurs. 8:30-7;
Tues. & Wed. 8:30-6; Fri. 8:30-5

The University of Illinois Bookstore in the Epi Center is open to the public and sells more than 20,000 titles of fiction and children's books as well as magazines and newspapers.

The store is wheelchair accessible. Because it is connected to the University, call ahead for the hours they are open.

Northern Suburbs

Abraham's Books

General

613 Dempster St.
Evanston, IL 60201
708-475-1777
Hours: Mon. Wed. 12-3;
Tues. Thurs. 12-5; Sat. 10-5

"I try to stock books that in ten years will endure the test of time," said Arnold Glass, owner of Abraham's Books.

The marvelously tall book shelves contain 12,000 used and antiquarian books addressing such topics as history, architecture, music, performing arts, philosophy, science, psychology, social sciences, fiction, militaria, photography and religion. Many of the books have gorgeous, ornate covers. Founded in 1979, the store is well organized.

Fortunately, Abraham's Books is wheelchair accessible and assistance is readily available for reaching the books on the higher shelves. Parking is on the street and mass transit is available.

The quality is good and the prices are reasonable, two good reasons to visit Abraham's Books.

Alkahest Bookshop

Antiquarian

1814 Central St.
Evanston, IL 60201
708-475-0990
Hours: Tues., Wed., Fri., Sat.
11-5; Thurs. 11-7; Sunday 1-5

"Off the Beaten Path," is the way the staff at Alkahest Bookshop describe their quality collection of more than 6,000 new and used, scholarly and out-of-print editions.

The store displays a selection of quality reprint editions. Other books are filed by category. Topics include history, Americana, general literary works, criticisms, fine art, anthropology, horror and fantasy fiction, children's books, illuminated books, and women's studies. They will conduct a search for any books you want to add to your collection.

You don't need to be an expert at book collecting to browse at Alkahest Bookshop. The staff is informed and happy to discuss books and show you books that will enhance your knowledge of book collecting. It's easy to recognize the value of many of the beautifully bound and gilded books. Quantity discounts can grow as large as 20%, depending upon your purchase.

The Alkahest Bookshop newsletter informs clients about recent acquisitions and includes articles about antiquarian book collecting. The store is wheelchair accessible. Off-street parking is available in a nearby Chicago Northwestern parking lot on weekends. Mass transit is also available.

American Opinion Book & Research

Conservative

1545 Waukegan Rd.
Glenview, IL 60025
708-724-0449
Hours: Wed. & Thurs. 10-8:30;
Sat. 10-2

A conservative, pro-American bookshop concerned with current events, the American Opinion Books and Research store is a haven filled with 1,000 new and used books, magazines, pamphlets, and brochures.

The store is staffed by volunteers who, according to a descriptive flyer from the store, "hold a common love of God, Family, Country, and a strong belief in the traditional values that are the cornerstone of this great nation." The store was established in 1964.

The literature available in the store covers biography, education, history, economics, health-nutrition, religion, foreign affairs and communism/socialism. Additional material for sale includes flags, audio-tapes, video-tapes, bumper stickers, letter stickers, and newsletters. Video tapes are for rent as well as for sale.

Off street parking is close. Physically, the tiny store has minimal space for a wheelchair but volunteers are pleased to help everyone. Clients come to the store from out-of-state. Mail orders are welcome.

The store motto is included on one of their flyers and reads, "We don't carry both sides, just the right side!"

Annie's Book Stop Inc.

Used
268 Hawthorn Village Commons
Vernon Hills, IL 60061
708-849-4774
Hours: Monday-Saturday 10-5;
Sunday 12-5

"Today's books---Yesterday's Prices," is the theme of Annie's Book Stop Inc. located in suburban Vernon Hills. In stock are thousands of "immaculate pre-read paperbacks at half the original cover price," adds Holly Sadowski of Annie's Book Stop Inc.

The topics are varied: fiction, cookery, romance, mystery, science fiction, humor, biography, arts and crafts, psychology, and children's books. They will order any book in print and will search for out-of-print books. Also for sale are country crafts and handmade clothing items, greeting cards, Cliff Notes, and reasonably priced gift items.

The folks at Annie's Book Stop want to make you comfortable by designing the store to be as cozy as your living room. They haven't forgotten the kids either. There is a special play and reading area for children. At times, children's story-telling time invites the kids to explore books.

Discounts abound at Annie's. All pre-read books are sold at half the cover cost. If you bring books to trade, you'll be given credit toward your next purchase. Vouchers for future use are available. You receive a free pre-read book for every ten books costing $1.00 or more that you purchase. But that's not all. Annie's Book Stop has special promotions that include 20% off a bag of books.

Open daily, Annie's Book Stop is wheelchair accessible and has off-street parking nearby. Mass transit is close. Annie's Pledge: "To treat our customers in such a way that they will want to return often."

Anthony Maita

Militaria
813 Greenwood Rd.
Glenview, IL 60025
708-998-9804
Hours: Mail order only

If you're looking for a militaria specialist, Anthony Maita is your man. He publishes a monthly listing of over 140 books with descriptions. The list includes new and used books, mostly hardbound. Topics range from history to biography, all with attention to the militaria theme.

To get onto his mailing list, send $1.25 to cover postage on four issues, to the above address. No subscription charge is made for those who order books.

Articles of War Ltd.

Militaria

8806 N. Bronx
Skokie, IL 60077
708-674-7445
Hours: Tues., Wed, Fri. 11-6;
Thurs. 11-9; Sat. 10-5

If you're searching for books about the military, Articles of War Ltd. is the place to start your reconnaissance. You'll find 10,000 books related to the military, history, and antiques. Some foreign language books in German, Spanish, and French discussing military affairs are available.

With twenty years of experience, owner Robert Ruman is a true military antiquarian and is able to share his wealth of information. His staff all have received special training from Bob regarding this highly specialized field. Special orders are no problem.

"During the last five years," Bob said, "there has been much more interest in the military field. It was slim at the end of the Vietnam War, but has changed now."

With 10,000 titles in stock, Articles of War Ltd. has especially strong selections about the Civil War, the Napoleonic era, World War II, Korea, the U.S. western expansion, American Indians and the Pony Express. For those who study warfare earlier than this, Bob stocks many books about ancient/medieval warfare.

Although the store is wheelchair accessible from the outside, it is not on the inside.

If it's a military flavor you like in your history books, do stop by Articles of War Ltd.

B. Dalton Bookseller

General

680 N. Western Ave.
Lake Forest, IL 60045
708-295-1107
Hours: Mon.-Sat. 9-5:30;
Sun. 12-4

B. Dalton Bookseller

General

708 Hawthorn Mall
Vernon Hills, IL 60061
708-362-4790
Hours: Mon.-Fri. 10-9;
Sat. 10-6; Sun. 11-5

B. Dalton Bookseller

General

203 Lakehurst Mall
Waukegan, IL 60085
708-473-0030
Hours: Mon.-Fri. 10-9;
Sat. 10-5; Sun. 11-5

Barat College Bookstore

Text

700 E. Westleigh Rd.
Lake Forest, IL 60045
708-295-4466
Hours: Mon.-Thurs. 10-6:30
(summer: Mon.-Thurs. 10-2)

In addition to textbooks, Barat College Bookstore sells school emblems, pennants, office supplies, greeting cards, and general trade reference books. The store is wheelchair accessible.

Beck's Book Store

Text, General

1041 Ridge Road
Wilmette, IL 60091
708-853-3080
Hours: Times vary when classes are in session- call ahead

This branch of Beck's Book Store is a resource for textbooks and supplies for students of Loyola/Mallinckrodt College. It is also open to the public and wheelchair accessible.

Best of Books

Religious

927 Ridge Road
Wilmette, IL 60091
708-256-5770
Hours: Mon.-Sat. 9-5:30

Best of Books sells Christian books about a wide range of topics: fiction, biography, education, history, games, psychology, romance, cookery, reference, sports, women's studies, archaeology, economics, health and nutrition, music, and science fiction. For the convenience of customers who have difficulty reading tiny print, they also stock many large type print books and books on recorded tape. Over 4,000 titles are in stock. Additional merchandise includes greeting cards, gifts, jewelry, and music tapes.

Christian music plays while you browse. Best of Books will gift wrap and mail purchases. The store is wheelchair accessible. Parking and mass transit are nearby. In 1992, the Best of Books will celebrate their twentieth year in business.

The Book Bin

General

1133 Church St.
Northbrook, IL 60062
708-498-4999
Hours: Mon.-Fri. 9-5:30;
Sat. 9-5; mail order

The Book Bin in the northern suburb of Northbrook has been in business for twenty years and has brought quality service and a good selection of new books to the community. Special orders are accepted at no extra charge. Special events include author autographing sessions and children's programs. There is also have a mail order service. The store is wheelchair accessible.

Book Fair, Inc.

Children's

1775 Chestnut Ste. I
Glenview, IL 60025
708-965-1466
Hours: Tues.-Sat. 11-5

The Book Stall at Chestnut Court

General

811 Elm St.
Winnetka, IL 60093
708-446-0882
Hours: Mon.-Sat. 9:30-5:30

"We cater to a community of the North Shore that cares for us as much as we care for them," said owner Roberta Rubin of her store, The Book Stall at Chestnut Court in Winnetka.

With over 37,000 titles, the book selection has something for everyone: fiction, history, photography, humor, horticulture, classics, fine art, cook books, women's studies, psychology, business and management, and children's books. The travel and tourism section is particularly extensive. Some books are printed in large type. In addition for sale are tee-shirts with book themes, audio and video tapes, and children's toys.

The services offered are also extensive. If you live in Winnetka, the Book Stall will deliver books right to your front door. They conduct children's activities, corporate gift services, in-store book fairs for schools, readings, book clubs, children's story telling, and author autographing. A book discussion group meets every Wednesday morning and is open to everyone. A list of books to be discussed is available in the store. Discussions are led by local university professors, editors, authors, and Book Stall reviewers.

The newsletter published by the Book Stall at Chestnut Court is a helpful buying guide. Each issue has many book reviews, the New York Times and Book Stall bestseller lists, a listing of soon-to-be-published books, new arrivals, special bookstore activities, and a column by owner Roberta Rubin.

Off-street parking is available as well as close mass transit. Because the store has narrow aisles, a raised section accessible only by stairs, and is typically very crowded, wheelchair users will not be able to fully enjoy The Book Stall. The entry is fully accessible, however.

Established in 1940, this bright store with general interest merchandise is easy to find and employees do their best to handle the large number of customers.

BOOKids

Children's   Hawthorn Center Mall
                                          Vernon Hills, IL

Scheduled to open Fall, 1991.

Bookman's Alley

General Antique   1712 (rear) Sherman Ave.
                                          Evanston, IL 60201
                                          708-869-6999
                                          Hours: Mon. 12-7; Thurs. 12-9;
                                          Tues.-Wed. 12-8; Fri.-Sun. 12-6

Bookman's Alley rings true to its name by having it's front door located in an Evanston alley. The maze design of the store is filled with over 35,000 used and antiquarian books in an atmosphere that is more like being in Grandpa's attic than a modern bookstore.

As you browse through the shelves, don't miss all the delightful details found everywhere. Intertwined with the books are authentic old bomber jackets, riding helmets, antique artwork, baskets, model ships, antique furniture, fedoras, Indian blankets, weathervanes, well-used baseball gloves, and even an old full-size printing press. The area near the records and old sheet music also is home for a piano, trumpet, and other instruments. Fresh flowers and thriving plants adorn all the wonderful little reading niches where people are invited to sit while investigating books.

If you love antiques and antique books, you'll think you're in book heaven at Bookman's Alley, which was established in 1980. This is the store most mentioned by other book store owners. Allocate a generous portion of your time when you visit Bookman's Alley. Even though the huge store is a maze of special zig-zags filled with books and knick-knacks, a wheelchair can maneuver around the store with only a few trouble spots.

Bookman's Alley does sponsor author autograph sessions and, for the entertainment of clients browsing, conducts live music performances. For the book shopper who loves treasure hunting, Bookman's Alley is a must.

Booknook Parnassus

Used

2000 Maple
Evanston, IL 60201
708-475-3445
Hours: Tues.-Fri. 11-6; Sat. 11-5

Located near other bookstores in Evanston, Book Parnassus is a used bookstore that features the humanities and fine arts. The shelves hold approximately 20,000 good used books.

One step to get into the store makes it difficult for wheelchairs.

The Bookworks

General

3441 Main
Evanston, IL 60202
312-871-5318
Hours: Mon.-Sat. 1-10;
Sun. noon-6

C.G. Jung Institute Bookstore

Psychology   550 Callan Ave.
                                                Evanston, IL 60202
                                                708-475-4848
                                                Hours: Mon., Wed.-Fri. 10-5;
                                                Tue., Sat. 10-4

One may expect that a bookstore directly associated with the C.G. Jung Institute would carry exclusively C.G. Jung material. Not so.

They carry more than 2,500 titles relating to analytical psychology, mythology, dreams, fairy tales, art and art therapy, spirituality, philosophy, women's studies, and the emerging subject of men's studies. In addition, they sell a selection of cards, calendars, and blank books. Members of the C.G. Jung Institute receive 10% store discounts. Special orders are welcome and often arrive in less than a week.

However, the bookstore is not wheelchair accessible and may be difficult if you have a little one in a stroller with you. There are ten steps to enter the store and the manager reports that it is not a readily accessible store within either. Fortunately, they do have a mail and phone order service.

As a description of the Institute, their literature states: "The C.G. Jung Institute of Chicago is a not-for-profit adult education center committed to the field of analytical psychology, begun by Carl Gustav Jung, and carried on by those who share common values and ideas about the psyche."

The Institute conducts educational programs on Jungian analysis for the general public whether they are beginners or advanced students of this field. They also have a referral service for people seeking Jungian analysis.

Carpenter's Shop

Religious   19056 W. Grand Ave.
                                                Lake Villa, IL 60046
                                                708-356-9575
                                                Hours: Mon.-Thurs. 10-6;
                                                Fri. 10-7:30; Sat. 10-5

Over 5,000 Christian books await you at the Carpenter's Shop in Lake Villa. Topics include Christian living, counseling, psychology, social sciences, devotionals, cults, fiction, theology, biographies, and prayer. Of course, they also sell many Bibles including a large type edition. Books on tape are available for many titles. Video rental and sales are also a service to customers. They also sell greeting cards, Precious Moments, and various gifts.

The Carpenter's Shop is wheelchair accessible and is open everyday except Sunday.

Chandler's Book Dept.

Used   630 Davis St.
                                            Evanston, IL 60204
                                            708-475-7200
                                            Hours: Mon.-Sat. 9-6; Thurs. 9-8

Located close to Northwestern University in Evanston, Chandler's is an Evanston institution. Their book department carries used textbooks as well as books in the following categories: fiction, history, metaphysics, mystery, romance, philosophy, cookery, women's studies, black studies, health and nutrition, local interest, religion, science fiction, and theatre.

They specialize in children's books, study guides, and student reference materials. Other learning items for sale include globes, maps, classical music tapes, puzzles, and stuffed animals.

Services, including great customer rapport, include laminating, copying, and printing. Customers may apply for a 10% courtesy discount card.

The old-fashioned elevator, operated by Kevin, located in the center of the store makes the book department accessible for strollers and wheelchairs. Off-street parking and mass transit are available.

Chicago Historical Bookworks

Used Science Fiction and Americana   831 Main St.
                                            Evanston, IL 60202
                                            708-869-6410
                                            Hours: Tues.-Wed., Fri.-Sat.
                                            11-6; Thurs. 11-9:30; Sun. 11-6

Just inside the door at Chicago Historical Bookworks is a yellow police ribbon stating, "Do not cross." Near the crime ribbon are a shelf of books about Chicago's history, both legal and otherwise. Some books are hardbound and focus on Illinois history, but a majority of the store features an extensive collection of used science fiction and fantasy paperbacks and magazines.

The store is wheelchair accessible but it is very difficult to maneuver inside.

If you are visiting Chicago and insist on finding some souvenir showing Al Capone, you may consider a book here titled: "Quotable Al Capone."

Coopersmith's

General   224 Hawthorne S/Ctr.
                                         Vernon Hills, IL 60061
                                         708-464-2278
                                         Hours: Mon.-Fri. 9-9;
                                         Sat. 10-6; Sun. 11-5

   If you have ever visited any of the three Coopersmith's branches, you
know that they have an outstanding book selection, beautiful gifts,
comfortable atmosphere, and terrific customer service.
   The largest of the three stores is located in Woodfield Mall in
Schaumburg. The Vernon Hills and North Michigan Avenue stores are
smaller. See the description of the Schaumburg store for more details.

Crown Books

General   1730 Sherman Ave.
                                         Evanston, IL 60201
                                         708-475-7776
                                         Hours: Mon., Thurs. 9-9;
                                         Tues., Wed, Fri, Sat 9-6;
                                         Sun. noon-5

Crown Books

General   661 Central Ave.
                                         Highland Park, IL 60035
                                         708-432-4640
                                         Hours: Mon.-Wed. 9-6; Sat. 9-6;
                                         Thurs., Fri. 9-9; Sun. 9-5;

Crown Books

General   8353 Golf Road
                                         Niles, IL 60648
                                         708-647-1997
                                         Hours: Mon.-Fri. 10-9;
                                         Sat. 10-6; Sun. 11-5

Crown Books

General   701 N. Milwaukee Ave.
                                                   Vernon Hills, IL 60061
                                                   708-816-1421
                                                   <u>Hours:</u> Mon.-Fri. 10-9;
                                                   Sat. 10-6; Sun. 11-5

Crown Books

General   92 S. Waukegan Rd.
                                                   Deerfield, IL 60015
                                                   708-498-5281
                                                   <u>Hours:</u> Mon.-Sat. 9-10;
                                                   Sun. 10-7

"If you paid full price you didn't buy it at Crown Books." We're all familiar with Robert M. Haft, President of Crown Books, saying this slogan in television commercials or printed advertisements. Though we tire quickly of slogans, this one is adhered to faithfully at all branches of Crown Books.

In the Chicago area, there are 43 locations (it increases every year) and all are open seven days per week. Discounts are found on every book and magazine on the shelves. New York Times hardcover best sellers are sold at 40% off the list price and paperbacks are 25% off. Computer best sellers are discounted 25%; books on tape at 20%; all other hardbacks at 20%; paperbacks and magazines at 10%. Typically, Crown outlets offer over 60 categories with 10,000 books available.

Many non-book items for sale include tote bags, calendars, blank video tapes, and gift bags. They do have a large children's section, often with children's cassette tapes stocked.

Crown Books often locates in a nearby strip-mall which means they are usually wheelchair accessible. Most everyone knows where to find their closest Crown Books. As a chain, they continue to grow in popularity.

D. J. Flynn-Books

Mail order
421 E. Westleigh Rd.
Lake Forest, IL 60045
708-234-1146
Hours: Mail order only

Doris Flynn's book business operates from her home by mail and phone order. She collects illustrated general out-of-print books and searches for books you can't find on your own. Also available are some paintings. Call her to receive special attention.

Europa Bookstore

Foreign Language
915 Foster St.
Evanston, IL 60201
708-866-6262
Hours: Mon.-Fri. 10-6; Sat. 10-5

If you habla espanol, parlez vous francais, or sprechen sie deutsche, you'll enjoy a visit to the Europa Bookstore. The store is totally devoted to foreign language books. You'll find 10,000 volumes written primarily in Spanish, French, German, and Italian. Books stocked include reference, fiction, literature, and children's books, along books teaching various foreign languages.

Instructors of foreign languages will find that the Europa Bookstore treats them as prized customers. Foreign language teachers network in the store and a ten percent discount is offered to teachers and school and university bookstores.

Although the store has no steps to make entry difficult for wheelchairs, there is not enough room inside the store to maneuver a wheelchair. The best you can do is wheel just inside the door, aisles are close with many items stacked on the floor.

George Ritzlin Maps and Books

Cartography, ABAA
469 Roger Williams Ave.
Highland Park, IL 60035
708-433-2627
Hours: Wed.-Fri. 12-6; Sat. 10-4;
Also appointments & mail order

As a side interest, many book lovers are turning to map collecting. Book lovers from all parts of the world contact George Ritzlin in

Highland Park. Not only are maps bits of living history, they adorn walls as prized works of art. For example, the walls of the Motorola Board Room are covered with original maps from the 1700's. Some maps are rough ink sketches made by an explorer or a highly artistic full color map with every line precisely entered on the page.

Since 1976, George has developed his hobby into a business that brings him pleasure and challenges. He has accumulated a fantastic collection of rare and antique maps. To find the treasured maps, George attends auctions and sometimes outsmarts the auctioneer with his knowledge. George is a member of the Antiquarian Booksellers Association of America with a specialization of cartography.

George and his wife have recently moved into a store in Highland Park after working for so many years from their home. The fresh, delightful store has over 2,000 collectible maps to offer to the public. George publishes a catalogue and special lists of maps. Prices range from $20 to over $7,000. Orders can be placed by telephone or mail but if you're nearby, you'll love to visit the store.

To the common man, a map is only good for finding roads from here to there. To the map enthusiast, maps are symbols of man's development. From the early explorers who did their best to estimate the size and shape of countries to space explorers who chart the earth from thousands of miles above the ground, maps have recorded our knowledge. Different types include navigational charts, waterway maps, city sketches with tiny buildings drawn in ink, celestial maps, and even humorous maps spoofing big city maps.

The Newberry Library in Chicago has an excellent collection of maps and supports the Chicago Map Association. Maps are often vital parts of their special exhibits.

Book lover's will find more than maps in George's store. He has a quality collection of reference books about maps for the beginner and enthusiast studying cartography. George is a distributor of "The Map Collector" magazine.

Maps aren't the only treasures found in George's store. He has an excellent collection of illuminated manuscripts actually set to paper by monks at surprisingly affordable prices. Many of the pieces are from the 15th century. Each one is different and shows the dedication of the artist to his work.

The store has one step to enter and is fully wheelchair accessible within.

George Ritzlin Maps and Books will inspire you to delve into this fascinating hobby, grow the passion you already have for maps, or to artistically decorate your home with a true conversation piece.

Giant Book Warehouse

General Discount

38971 N. Lewis
Zion, IL 60099
708-249-5000
<u>Hours:</u> Mon.-Fri. 10-7;
Sat. 10-6; Sun. 12-5

"You never know what we'll have but you'll love what you find," says Jordan Madorsky, owner of Giant Book Warehouse located two miles west of Illinois Beach State Park near the corner of Wadsworth and Lewis.

As a book lover, you'll thoroughly enjoy browsing for hours at Giant Book Warehouse. The books cover a broad general interest and are always changing. You can count on 50-95% discounts on new books. Jordan quickly points out that there are no text books included in the collection.

The Giant Book Warehouse is wheelchair accessible and open every day of the week. They are open for extended hours at holiday-time. Many customers travel for miles to shop at this store. Some people bring visiting friends from out-of-state to enjoy the Giant Book Warehouse as if it were a tourist attraction.

According to Jordan, this is the first bookstore in the Midwest to drastically discount new books. With discounts like these, it's easy to fill up three or four grocery bags full of books. Your neighbors might think you are carrying in groceries, and in a sense you are toting brain food.

Glencoe Book Shop Inc.

General

366 Park Ave.
Glencoe, IL 60022
708-835-4727
<u>Hours:</u> Mon.-Sat. 9-5:15;
mail order

Owner Raina Ruskin says the Glencoe Book Shop is a cozy oldtime book shop. Over 4,000 titles line the shelves. Topics range from the classics to cookery.

The 500 square foot store was established in 1970 and is wheelchair accessible. Authors occasionally visit to autograph their books. Special orders are welcome. Glencoe Book Shop also offers a mail order service.

Great Expectations

Scholarly

911 Foster St.
Evanston, IL 60201
708-864-3881
Hours: Mon.-Fri. 11-7; Sat. 11-6

Established in 1949, Great Expectations is the undisputed champion of academic philosophy books in the United States. They publish a monthly booklet describing their many new arrivals and sale books in philosophy for those unfortunate out-of-towners who can't visit the store. Orders for books in stock are normally shipped out within 24 hours. The store is so busy, they now ship books twice a day.

Proud of their philosophy collection, Great Expectations is filled with other excellent departments: science (especially physics), economics, music and theatre. They also offer a variety of publishers classic collections and literary critical essays. There are between 65-75,000 books in stock.

You don't have to look far to find Penguins; Penguin Publications that is. However, you may do a double take when you see the store cat sleeping in the window and another cat dozing in a corner.

All books are new, crisp and filed in an organized, cool atmosphere. The store is wheelchair accessible except for one group of classics located up four steps in the back of the store. Friendly employees are available to help. Parking is on the street and not so difficult to find as it is in Chicago. Mass transit is close.

Located on a shady, tree-lined street in Evanston, Great Expectations certainly fulfills anyone's expectations. Great Expectations is very customer oriented. They claim that without their valued customers they might as well change their name to Bleak House or Hard Times. If you can't visit, be sure to write for a catalogue. This is a superb bookstore.

Green Earth

Health & Nutrition

2545 Prairie Ave.
Evanston, IL 60201
708-864-8949
Hours: Daily 10-7

"We have the best selection of books about health and nutrition in the area," says buyer John Kilbourne. "Other book stores often refer customers to us."

Green Earth was established in 1970 and also carries books about food allergies, acupuncture, vegetarianism, self-help, and the healing arts. Non-book items include foods.

The store is wheelchair accessible and maintains a friendly rapport with customers. They are pleased to help clients find the food and books that keep them happy and healthy.

Hamakor Gallery, Ltd.

Religious, Hebrew

4150 Dempster
Skokie, IL 60076
708-966-4040
Hours: Sun. 10-5; Fri. 10-3;
Mon. & Thurs. 10-9;
Tues. & Wed. 10-5:30

Hebrew and Jewish books are the highlight of the Hamakor Gallery, Ltd. and over 1000 titles are in stock. Located in suburban Skokie, the store was established in 1950. With Jewish-Israeli music playing, you'll also find Jewish art, gifts, invitations, and jewelry.

Off-street parking is available, mass transit is close, and the store is wheelchair accessible. The store is open every day except Saturday.

Hamill & Barker

Antiquarian, ABAA

1719 Howard St.
Evanston, IL 60202
708-475-1724
Hours: Mon.-Fri. 9-4:30; Sat.
10-4; August by appointment

Rare books and first editions are found at Hamill & Barker, book antiquarians supreme. Located in Evanston, they carry 15,000 books in a 2,500 square foot store.

Terence A. Tanner, proprietor, notes that they carry rare books printed in the 1500's, when books were first printed using movable type. Their rare books encompass all fields and are in many different languages. Other books available include Americana, Chicago and Illinois history, medicine, science, technology, architecture, and literature.

The store is wheelchair accessible with off-street parking available and mass transit close.

If you're looking for rare manuscripts or maps and prints of Chicago and Illinois, call Hamill & Barker. You'll be pleased with their selection.

Herbert Furse - Bookman

Antiquarian

1461 Baffin Rd.
Glenview, IL 60025
708-724-4594
Hours: Appointment or mail
order only

A Dickens scholar, Herbert Furse has a general interest collection of antique and out-of-print books. Herbert participates in book fairs and sells quite a bit to book dealers.

Historical Newspapers & Journals

History

9850 Kedvale
Skokie, IL 60076
708-676-9850
Hours: Appointment only

Steve and Linda Alsberg love yesterday's news. Actually, they own and operate Historical Newspapers and Journals on Kedvale in Skokie. Their impressive newspapers are dated from 1670 through the 1940's.

You can view the collection by calling for an appointment. Steve notes that they're easiest to reach during evenings and weekends. A mutually convenient time can be set up.

In addition to historical newspapers, they have a collection of autographed material from past United States Presidents, scientists, authors, and musicians that are available for purchase. Also for sale are early maps, wood engravings, and color illustrations. Each piece is unique and truly a treasure.

A mail order catalogue is available if you're unable to meet the Alsbergs.

J.T. Monckton Ltd.

Travel

1050 Gage Street
Winnetka, IL 60093
708-446-1106
Hours: Call-hours differ

Travel is the main focus of the books carried by J.T. Monckton Ltd. You'll also find many antique maps and prints available. Be sure to call before visiting J.T. Monckton Ltd. because hours do differ.

Kay's Treasured Kookbook Kollection

Mail order

P.O. Box 17
Kenilworth, IL 60043
708-256-1773
<u>Hours:</u> Mail order only

Kay's Treasured Kookbook Kollection is one of the most unique book businesses in the Chicago area. What ingredients make it so unique?

Take one cooking enthusiast, Kay Sullivan, add a passion for finding new recipes, and stir in a lot of energy. Serve garnished with many people who love to cook and collect.

Kay searches every corner for and has a collection of over 3,000 out-of-print cookbooks herself. The oldest in her personal library is dated 1790.

"The most gratifying part of my business is all the nice folks I meet," said Kay. She has customers from all parts of the United States and Canada. Two of her former Chicago clients have moved to Switzerland and still order books from Kay. She adds that she has ten clients in Alaska.

The most requested cookbooks are Betty Crocker titles and Farm Journal although ethnic and regional cookbooks remain popular. Kay is proud that she has a 95% success rate in her cookbook searching. She says that people collect cookbooks to complete a series, replace well-worn books, or as sentimental gifts.

To find many of the cookbooks, Kay travels to house sales, flea markets, book fairs and examines shelf upon shelf of used bookstores. She also is a part of a book collectors' network system.

Kay's cooking expertise may soon be available to everyone. She has plans to write her own cookbook of family favorites. It's sure to be a well-thumbed cookbook for many people.

Kenneth Nebenzahl Inc.

Antiquarian, ABAA

P.O. Box 370
Glencoe, IL 60022
708-835-0515
<u>Hours:</u> Appointment only

A member of the Antiquarian Booksellers' Association of America, Kenneth Nebenzahl specializes in Americana, Maps, Astronomy, and History.

Kroch's & Brentano's Inc.

General

1711 Sherman Avenue
Evanston, IL 60201
708-328-7220
Hours: Mon. & Thurs. 9:30-9;
Tues., Wed., Fri., Sat. 9:30-5:30;
Sun. noon-5

Kroch's & Brentano's Inc.

General

36 Old Orchard Center
Skokie, IL 60077
708-674-7550
Hours: Mon.-Fri. 10-9;
Sat. 10-6; Sun. 11-5

Kroch's & Brentano's Inc.

General

106 Hawthorn Center
Vernon Hills, IL 60061
708-367-0141
Hours: Mon.-Fri. 10-9;
Sat. 10-6; Sun. 11-5

Lake Forest Bookstore Inc.

General

624 N. Western Ave.
Lake Forest, IL 60045
708-234-4420
Hours: Mon.-Sat. 9-5:30

North Shore Magazine named Lake Forest Bookstore as the best bookstore on the north shore. With 30,000 books on the shelves, every shopper is sure to find a book of interest here.

The topics run the full gamut of interests including fiction, biography, history, travel, fine art, cookery, cinema, local interest, and children's books. Some books are available in large type print and on audio tape. Non-book items for sale are plush toys accenting popular children's books, greeting cards, video tapes, and wrapping paper.

Lake Forest Bookstore was established in 1950. Services the store offers are special ordering of books, shipping, and operating a rental library. The store is wheelchair accessible and seating is available as you browse the full book shelves. Off street parking makes visiting this bookstore easy.

Lake Forest College Bookstore

Text

Sheridan Rd. Commons Bldg.
Lake Forest, IL 60045
708-234-7240
Hours: Mon. 8-6;
Tues.-Fri. 8-4:30

Basically intended for students, the Lake Forest College Bookstore is open to the public and sells a small selection of reference and fiction in addition to textbooks. They also carry the usual college items: emblem clothes, assorted gifts, greeting cards, and posters. The store is not wheelchair accessible.

Leekley Books

Antiquarian

P.O. Box 337
Winthrop Harbor, IL 60096
708-872-2311
Hours: Appointment only

Following a love for books developed in him by his father, Brian Leekley collects scholarly out-of-print books. His father founded the business in 1961 and Brian joined the tradition in 1978.

The business operates by appointment only or through mail and telephone orders. He can be found at his book stand at the Midwest Book Hunters Book Faire.

Lemstone Books

Religious

401 Hawthorn Center
Vernon Hills, IL 60061
708-367-7100
Hours: Mon.-Fri. 10-9;
Sat. 10-6; Sun. 11-5

113

Literati & Company

Mail order

P.O. Box 1526
Highland Park, IL 60035
708-432-0346
Hours: Mail order only

"For the facts of life, read fiction," is the motto of Literati & Company's President Gary Giuntoli.

To make book shopping easy, Literati & Company is a phone and mail order business that offers discounts to clients. If you order a number of books, your discount increases.

Literati & Company works closely with big businesses that have their own libraries or offer book savings to their employees. Searches for specific titles in a wide variety of topics are no problem for Literati & Company.

Whether you're interested in finding a technical computer book or the hot titles in fiction, Literati & Company can assist you.

Logos of Evanston

Religious

820 Davis St.
Evanston, IL 60201
708-864-3030
Hours: Mon.-Wed., Fri. 10-6:30;
Thurs. 10-8; Sat. 9:30-5

Marshall Field & Co. Book Dept.

General

One Old Orchard
Skokie, IL 60077
708-674-1234
Hours: Mon.-Fri. 10-9;
Sat. 10-5; Sun. 11-6

Marytown Gift Shop

Religious   1600 W. Park Ave.
Libertyville, IL 60048
708-367-7800
Hours: Mon.-Sat. 9-5

Marytown Gift Shop is a Catholic bookstore with approximately 1,500 titles, some of which they publish themselves. The store is wheelchair accessible and is open six days per week.

The Memorabilia Corner

Antiquarian   3677A Washington Ave.
Great Lakes, IL 60088
708-473-9688
Hours: Appointment and mail order only

For the past eighteen years, The Memorabilia Corner has carried approximately 10,000 books about antiques, history, and genealogy. The store conducts business by mail order only,

Missions Possible Bookstore

Religious   400 E. Westminster Rd.
Lake Forest, IL 60045
708-234-4760
Hours: Sept-June: Mon.-Fri. 10-4; Sat. 10-noon;
July & August: Mon.-Fri. 10-1; Sat. 10-noon

"We are a full service bookstore specializing in religious, social, self-help, and women's issues," says Linda H. Illes of Missions Possible.

They also offer a selection of children's books, large type print books, and music. Book titles in stock number 1,800. Non-book items are religion-oriented and include jewelry, folk art, nativity scenes, framed calligraphy, and greeting cards.

Although Missions Possible is located in Church of the Holy Spirit, an Episcopal church, the focus is ecumenical and appropriate to all religions. Discounts are extended to the clergy and non-profit agencies.

The store is wheelchair accessible. Missions Possible is staffed by volunteers.

National Louis University Bookstore

Text

2840 Sheridan
Evanston, IL 60201
708-256-5150
Hours: Mon.-Fri. 9-6; Sat. 10-1

Nevermore Books

Used

1224 Asbury Ave.
Winnetka, IL 60093
708-446-7187
Hours: Mail, Phone, or Appt.

Sharon Morgan Blakley and her husband, Richard, can't get enough of books. When travelling, they have passed up some of America's historic areas just to stop at used bookstores. Because of their sacrifice, you benefit. Sharon and Richard operate Nevermore Books which is a mail-order service specializing in used and out-of-print mysteries, crime, suspense, espionage, and detective fiction. Both hardbacks and paperbacks are stocked. For the collector, they carry first editions, author autographed copies, and reading copies.

They publish a catalogue twice per year highlighting their stock of over 5,000 books and will happily find any book in their field that you may want. They also assist with special orders. They are happy to open their shelves for inspection on an appointment basis.

"In this field, many books are off the shelves and out-of-print within a year," explained Sharon. "When awards are given, books are sometimes no longer available."

Sharon and Richard attend many conventions for book lovers and know many authors themselves. They are delightful people who happily discuss the mystery genre. Their expertise is a mere phone call away.

New Words of Wisdom Books Ltd. Inc.

Religious

1722 Milwaukee Ave.
Glenview, IL 60025
708-298-9306
Hours: Tues.-Thurs. 9:30-6;
Fri. 9:30-9; Sat. 9-5

This new store, New Words of Wisdom Books, located in Glenview, carries over 2,500 titles of religious books, musical tapes, video tapes,

116

pictures, gifts, and greeting cards. The religious books are influenced by Mormon and Latter Day Saints theology.

If you're looking for the perfect wedding announcements, this book store can help you choose the beautiful wedding remembrances for you and the guests.

The store is wheelchair accessible and parking is nearby. During weekdays, mass transit is available. The store was established in 1989.

Norma K. Adler Books

Antiquarian   59 Eastwood Dr.
                                           Deerfield, IL 60015
                                           708-945-8575
                                           Hours: Appointment only

Whatever book you would like, call Norma K. Adler, antiquarian. She'll search and find the book you desire. Her business operates by appointment only.

Norma is especially proud of her book searches in the fields of fiction, literature and biography.

Peking Book House

Chinese   1520 Sherman Ave.
                                           Evanston, IL 60201
                                           708-491-0477
                                           Hours: Mon.-Sat. 10-7; Sun. 3-6

After enjoying your visit to Peking Book House, you may want to investigate the other two branches. Make sure you have your passport because the two other branches are located in China. Owner Chen Chan Cheng operates the bookstores in China near his hometown of Yumping.

If you can't travel to China, be sure to visit the Evanston Peking Book House which was established in 1971. Between the quality of the 20,000 titles of books on the seven-foot tall shelves and the wonderful personality of Mr. Cheng, it's difficult to say which is the shining star of the shop.

Only about one-fifth of the books are written in Chinese or Japanese. Most of the customers speak English as their main language. The books are a personal library for Mr. Cheng. The main topics include history, philosophy, cookery, health and nutrition, medicine, meditation, religion, travel and tourism, black studies, women's studies, children's books, literature, and fiction.

The small store also stocks abacuses, acupuncture kits, mah-jong games, stuffed panda bears, origami greeting cards, and so much more.

Mr. Cheng was born in 1926 in the mountain section of southern China. During his life he has experienced the Japanese invasion of China, a school revolt against a principal who embezzled government funds, a stint in the Youth Army, the Communist take-over, exile in Taiwan, and eventual immigration to America.

Here, he is a happy man who has been an inspiration to many. His customers are all his friends and no one enters without becoming a friend. Mr. Cheng's enthusiasm about life makes the atmosphere of Peking Book House a lively and invigorating one. In the philosophy of Taoism, water which flows and is flexible and yielding overcomes that which is hard. Mr. Cheng has flowed with the high and low tides of his life and delightfully shares his philosophy with those who stop at the store.

Be sure to experience Peking Book House. You may take home a smile on your face as well as a shelf of new books.

Pied Piper Children's Bookstore

Children's

603 Elm Place
Highland Park, IL 60035
708-433-6421
Hours: Mon.-Wed., Fri. 10-6;
Thurs. 10-8; Sat. 10-5

Just as the Pied Piper of children's literature enticed children to follow him, you'll find yourself and your children drawn to the Pied Piper Children's Bookstore in Highland Park.

Proprietors Tom and Elaine Tredinnick have developed a children's bookstore that really cares about children and lets them know that they're special people. The bright and airy store is lined with kid-height bookshelves filled with over 5,000 titles covering literature, games, science, sports, puzzles, globes, stuffed animals and greeting cards. Also offered are a selection of books in foreign languages, such as Humpty Dumpty in French.

It's not just the terrific selection of books that makes Pied Piper Children's Bookstore special, it's all the extras that make this store unique. The children of Ms. Hermann's Braeside School first grade class made a quilt (with some parents' help) and wrote a collection of descriptive essays about the quilt. Both are on display at Pied Piper.

The store sponsors a reading challenge program which encourages children to read. Each team of children reads specific books and participates in a question and answer game. Pied Piper Children's Bookstore also sponsors children's story telling and author autographing sessions. They even have a play area and carpeted steps for the child to climb and be at an even height with adults at the check-out counter.

While the children browse through their books, parents can brush up with a collection of parenting books. As an extra service, Pied Piper Children's Bookstore will special order any book in print. With time sparse for today's parents, this makes for one-stop-shopping for parents and children.

A newsletter keeps everyone informed about the special activities and recently acquired books. A catalogue of many of their books is available for the phone shopper.

The store is easy to find, has close parking, and is totally wheelchair accessible. Pied Piper Children's Bookstore is a Highland Park delight you shouldn't miss.

Platypus Bookshop

General

606 Dempster St.
Evanston, IL 60202
708-866-8040
Hours: Mon.-Sat. 10-6;
Thurs. 10-8; Sun. 12-4

Platypus has bookcases filled with 10,000 titles. Large departments include African-American, Native American, astrology, and parenting. Other departments carry books about psychology, fiction, literature, environment, Eastern philosophy and poetry. The children's section is up a large step and not easy for wheelchairs to maneuver in.

Platypus Bookshop is tight on space and wheelchairs can squeeze by and turn corners if leg rests are not on the wheelchair. Parking and mass transit are close. The store offers a ten percent discount for ten or more copies of a single title.

"We attempt to provide an open, pro-people atmosphere and share a liberal philosophy with our customers," said Margret Schnabel, owner of Platypus Bookshop. "For example, we carry pro-choice, feminist, peace activities, etc."

The store utilizes bulletin boards to keep customers informed of activities and reading groups in the area.

Preservation Bookshop (The Book Den)

Used

814 Dempster
Evanston, IL 60202
708-864-4449
Hours: Open Everyday; Hours
are flexible; Call ahead.

Describing his bookstore, owner Dave Wilhelm said, "This is a casual kind of store without being dingy and dusty."

The used books total over 10,000 and cover a variety of subjects: best-sellers in hardback and paperback covers, literature, science fiction, mystery and history. Also included are books about tattooing and underground comics. Dave is interested in buying and selling used books.

The store is wheelchair accessible, mass transit is close, but parking is on the street and can be tight at times. When you visit this bookshop, you may be fortunate enough to be greeted by a delightful shop cat.

Renaissance Books

Mail order

P. O. Box 954
Lincolnshire, IL 60069
708-634-9210
Hours: Mail order only

Juanita Shearer is one of the very few people who search for books on a full-time basis. She's been in business for twenty years and says that books are becoming harder to find as the years go by. Computers are becoming a part of the book search world.

Juanita keeps a small stock of collector books and will hunt for any book you desire from private press books to rare first and limited editions. Renaissance Books is a mail order business.

Richard S. Barnes

Antiquarian

1745 Hinman Avenue
Evanston, IL 60201
708-869-2272
Hours: Mail order only

An antiquarian who specializes in humanities and scholarly books, Richard S. Barnes conducts business by phone and mail order. He is a member of the Midwest Bookhunters and has made books his business for forty years. A catalogue is available.

Scotland Yard Books Ltd.

Mystery

556 Green Bay Road
Winnetka, IL 60093
708-446-2214
Hours: Monday-Saturday 9-5

Step into Scotland Yard Books and you step into a world of mystery with the flavor of the British Isles. The King stands in the back of the store pondering the question, "Why doesn't everyone read mystery books?" Who is the King? Sherlock Holmes dressed in his traditional wool coat and distinctive hat. The question: a true mystery.

Located in north suburban Winnetka, Scotland Yard Books carries virtually all paperback mystery titles available in print, has a beautiful large selection of hardcover books, and a shelf of used mysteries in good condition. The stock includes over 2,000 titles and was established in 1987.

Changing trends in mystery writing are noted here. Some books are published by feminist presses and some are direct imports from England. They also special order books and will take care of the mailing for you.

Special activities abound at Scotland Yard Books. Discussion groups are conducted approximately every six weeks and are open to everyone. Sherlock Holmes seminars are held and the store has a resident Sherlock Holmes expert. A writer's group, the Red Herrings, began in the store five years ago and continues to grow stronger. The group is a support group for fledgling mystery writers. One writer has graduated to the big time and is the current celebrity of Scotland Yard Books: Ron Levitsky published his first novel titled "The Love That Kills." The store also carries a variety of mystery newspapers, holds author autographing sessions, and maintains a bulletin board of activities and photographs from past to present. A newsletter is published to keep clients aware of activities.

This highly attractive store is conducive to browsing and is well-organized which you will especially appreciate if you only have a minute to dash inside. The store is completely wheelchair accessible because floor-to-ceiling rich wood bookcases line the walls leaving the huge center section open for a polished wooden table and chairs and a table of highlighted books. The British theme is carried throughout the store from the beautiful plaid carpeting to the red-coated statues of British soldiers on the top of bookcases. Yes, Sherlock's pipe is sitting on a shelf lined with books about him.

The staff is terrific. A requirement for employment is being well-read in the mysteries. A philosophy they share is finding the right book to suit the customer's tastes.

Back to the question, "Why doesn't everyone read mystery books?" If everyone visited Scotland Yard Books they would be inspired to delve into the mystery genre. This is a delightful store.

Second Editions

Used & New

7951 Babb Ave.
Skokie, IL 60077
708-677-0680
Hours: Mon.- Wed., Fri.
9:30-5:30; Thurs. 9:30-8;
Sat. 9:30-5; mail order

Second Editions is guarded by Merlin the cat who also publishes a newsletter about the store called "Cat Tales." In stock are 30-40,000 titles of new and used books in fiction, mystery, and science fiction. They have a strong mail order business.

The store is not wheelchair accessible.

Titles Inc.

Antiquarian, ABAA

1931 Sheridan Rd.
Highland Park, IL 60035
708-432-3690
Hours: Mon.-Sat. 10:30-5

Being the book person you are, you must, really must, stop in at Titles, Inc. in Highland Park to meet Florence Shay, the monarch of antiquarian books.

Florence conducts court in a shop she prefers to think of as a part of her home. The walls are lined with mahogany built-in bookcases and antique tables display luscious leather bound books to treasure. The store is comfortably carpeted and classical music soothes the browsing customer. Her desk is a library table surrounded with high-back leather swivel chairs conducive for chatting with the very personable Florence.

Antiquarian bookshops reflect the owner and at Titles, Inc. you'll find delightful treasures. Florence gathers a wide variety of topics and enjoys searching for special books customers want. In stock, she carries beautiful book sets bound in leather and topics including the fine arts, Chicago, theatre, literature, cookery, and children's books. Florence is a member of the Antiquarian Booksellers' Association of America.

Many of her books are purchased by book-lovers who just love to own rare first editions, signed copies, and obscure titles. Some do not read the books they buy; the pleasure comes in possessing the jewels.

Those who do read the rare books they purchase gain insights into history. She has sold a first edition medical textbook by Louis Pasteur, the first edition (dated 1791) of Boswell's "Life of Samuel Johnson," and a four-volume set about Abraham Lincoln written and signed by Carl Sandburg.

To qualify for Florence's shelves, a book must be in like-new condition with dust jackets unmarred and pages unthumbed. She has a keen eye for choosing fascinating volumes which carry price tags from very affordable to the thousands of dollars.

Unless a popular book is an early book of a renowned author and not readily available, it won't be on Florence's shelves.

While you're perusing the shelves, don't forget to keep an eye on who is standing next to you. Famous clients have included author Gay Talese, Chicago-born playwright David Mamet and author/illustrator Maurice Sendak who consulted Florence when he was designing the set for Mozart's "The Magic Flute."

As the chairwoman of the Midwest chapter of the Antiquarian Booksellers Association of America, Florence is in tune with a huge networking system. She often advises customers who are looking for people to re-bind antique books or restore damaged pages.

Titles Inc. is usually wheelchair accessible but when I visited, many books were piled in the aisles making it impossible for wheelchairs. Both parking and mass transit are available.

If you love and admire books, visit Titles, Inc. and meet owner Florence Shay. Even if you have never thought of book collecting as your personal passion, once you see her collection of treasures available, you won't be able to resist the urge to collect.

Trinity Beacon Bookstore

Religious

2065 Half Day Rd.
Deerfield, IL 60015
708-317-6800
Hours: Mon., Thurs. 9-7;
Tues., Wed., Fri. 9-5:30; Sat. 9-5

With gospel music playing, the Trinity Beacon Bookstore invites people to browse through their selection of Bibles (some written in Greek and Hebrew), religious books, printed music, recorded music, gifts, church curriculum, greeting cards, and office supplies. There are over 11,000 titles. Imprinting and gift wrapping is a special service to customers.

Radio remotes are conducted linking the store with recording artists and educational workshops. A newsletter describes the details of the special events.

The store is wheelchair accessible and seating is available within the store. Off-street parking is available.

WaldenKids

Children's

Northbrook Court
Northbrook, IL 60062
708-205-0044
Hours: Mon.-Fri 10-9;
Sat. 10-5:30; Sun. 12-5

Waldenbooks

General

Carillon Square
Glenview, IL 60025
708-998-9140
Hours: Mon.-Fri. 10-9;
Sat. 10-5:30; Sun. 12-5:30

Waldenbooks

General

Golf Mill Center Unit A-251
Niles, IL 60648
708-824-2218
Hours: Sun. 11-5;
Mon.-Sat. 10-9

Waldenbooks

General

1054 Northbrook Court
Northbrook, IL 60062
708-498-3475
Hours: Mon.-Fri. 10-9;
Sat. 10-5:30; Sun. 12-5:30

Waldenbooks

General

10077 Skokie Blvd.
Skokie, IL 60077
708-673-4007
<u>Hours:</u> Mon.-Fri. 10-9;
Sat. 10-5:30; Sun. 11-5

Waldenbooks

General

198 Lakehurst Ctr.
Waukegan, IL 60085
708-473-3353
<u>Hours:</u> Mon.-Fri. 10-9;
Sat. 10-5:30; Sun. 11-5

Waukegan Bridge Center

Bridge

927 Grand Ave.
Waukegan, IL 60085
708-662-7204
<u>Hours:</u> Call for hours

No, the Waukegan Bridge Center doesn't sell books about bridges. They do offer around 1,500 titles dealing with games, especially the card game of bridge.

Owner Bill Sachen notes that most of the books in stock are out-of-print selections. They do free book searches with no obligations on the part of the customer.

You'll also find autobridge, duplicate bridge boards and miscellaneous supplies as well as books about chess, backgammon, and other card games.

The store is wheelchair accessible with parking and mass transit close. Catalogues are issued with mail orders available.

For bridge lovers, Waukegan Bridge Center is heaven.

Wee the People of the World

Children's Antiquarian

408 Greenbay Rd., PO Box 142
Kenilworth, IL 60043
708-256-7944
Hours: Appointment and mail
order only

Antiquarian books don't just include the classics. Wee the People of the World bookshop specializes in antiquarian children's books and carries old, new, and used children's books.

Operating by mail order and appointment since 1978, Wee the People of the World publishes two types of catalogues. Each fall they print an illustrated color catalogue describing the best in new children's books just in time for holiday gift buying. The catalogue costs $2.00.

Their other publication is an antiquarian newsletter listing out-of-print and collectible books for sale. Some books include the author's autograph. Cost for this catalogue is $1.00.

Mary Wong, manager of Wee the People of the World, also stocks a small number of books specializing in the game of chess.

Discounts are available for schools and antiquarian dealers.

Northwest Suburbs

A Child's Garden of Books

Children's

P.O. Box 7108
147 McHenry Rd.
Buffalo Grove, IL 60089
708-537-5322
Hours: Mon.-Thurs. 10-9;
Fri. 10-6; Sat. 10-5;
Sept.-May: Sun. 12:30-5

"In our store you will find a book for every child in your life," says Tim Sroka, owner of A Child's Garden of Books in Buffalo Grove.

In addition to nurturing 2,500 different books in this garden, you'll find a harvest of other delights for your child. Offered is a large selection of children's music, many classical, handmade cloth books, wooden puzzles, and locally made dolls.

With children shoppers in mind, story telling happens twice every week. The needs of parents are not forgotten since the store provides a special club membership affording 10% discounts. Live music and author autographing are also some of the special events happening at A Child's Garden of Books.

This delightful children's book store is totally wheelchair and stroller accessible. Rest rooms are available for patrons and are also wheelchair accessible.

When school is in session, A Child's Garden of Books opens its doors on Sundays also.

B. Dalton Bookseller

General

475 Ela Rd. & Rt. 22
Lake Zurich, IL 60047
708-438-0112
Hours: Mon.-Fri. 9:30-5;
Sat. 9:30-6; Sun. 12-5

B. Dalton Bookseller

General   Woodfield Mall
                                Schaumburg, IL 60173
                                708-330-0660
                                Hours: Mon.-Fri. 10-9;
                                Sat. 10-6; Sun. 10-5

B. Dalton Bookseller

General   1338 Spring Hills Mall
                                West Dundee, IL 60118
                                708-428-6650
                                Hours: Mon.-Fri. 10-9;
                                Sat. 10-6; Sun. 11-5

Beyond Tomorrow Science Fiction & Comics

Science Fiction   815 East Dundee Rd.
                                Palatine, IL 60067
                                708-705-6633
                                Hours: Mon.-Fri. 11-8;
                                Sat. 11-6; Sun. 12-5

David Pregozen wanted to create a bookstore that he, as a customer, would like to shop in. He's done just that. You'll also enjoy leisurely browsing the 5,000 book titles in stock, partaking of the friendly atmosphere where questions are fully answered, and maybe joining in a discussion about science fiction, horror, and fantasy books.

"It is as much a meeting place as it is a store, people with common interests, spending time together," David says.

But that's not all. David added another of his interests to his store-- comics. 12-15,000 comic books are in stock; many are new, many are back issues.

"We are fully committed to the comic industry as a whole, not just the popular times," David explains. "We see comics as its own unique medium, not just as a waiting ground for movies or TV. We stock the full range of this story-telling medium."

In addition to reading material, David stocks T-shirts, posters, toys, trading cards, and supplies necessary to maintaining the quality of comics and trading cards. Discounts are given to members of the store's subscription service. Special orders are no problem and a catalogue is published. The store is wheelchair accessible. Authors visit the store for autographing sessions.

Beyond Tomorrow Science Fiction and Comics leaves the high-tech concept of bookselling behind and builds a world where friendliness and an extensive stock join with information and service to make a quality store.

The Book Rack

Used

213 W. Dundee Rd.
Buffalo Grove, IL 60089
708-537-6633
Hours: Sat. 10:30-6; Sun. 12-4;
Mon.-Wed. 11-6;Thurs.-Fri. 11-8

The Book Vine for Children

Children's

304 Lincoln Ave.
Fox River Grove, IL 60021
708-639-4220
Hours: Mon. 9-5;
Tues.-Fri. 9-6; Sat. 10-4

Who better to manage a children's bookstore than two former children's librarians? Both owners of The Book Vine for Children, Liz Smith and Isabel Baker, began their careers in just that way.

In addition to selling children's books to schools and libraries, Liz and Isabel conduct book fairs in schools. Although they are primarily wholesalers, they do operate a retail store open to everyone.

The store is wheelchair and stroller accessible but Liz notes that when Book Fair season is on, the store has boxes of books all over the place!

Established in 1988, the store has approximately 2,500 titles and over 8,000 books in stock. Many books are multicultural. In addition to books, The Book Vine for Children offers storytelling cassettes. A ten percent discount is given to teachers. Telephone and mail orders are welcome.

The Christian Shop, Ltd.

Religious   Fox Fire Mall, Rand & Hicks
                                              Palatine, IL 60067
                                              708-991-8994
                                              Hours: Mon.-Thurs. 9:30-8;
                                              Fri. Sat. 9:30-5

In a store named The Christian Shop you know you'll find Bibles, Bible study aids, and Bible reference books but you'll also find other treasures.

All of their books are by Christian publishers and the topics include fiction, church history, psychology, romance, women's studies, health-nutrition, music, cookery, humor, magazines, and children's books. Some books are printed in Spanish and there are large print books available. The Christian Shop stocks over 2,500 different titles.

Other items for sale are Christian music, "Precious Moments" figurines, and the Carry Edna Hible collection of plates and prints.

Services include gift wrapping, mailings, and telephone orders. If you are a senior citizen, you'll receive a discount in prices on Wednesdays. At times, you'll be able to meet authors of your favorite books during autograph sessions. At other times, you may enjoy live music in the store.

To describe the store's philosophy, Susan Rheaume said, "In an ambience of serenity enhanced by Christian background music, we strive to provide information which will reinforce individual's spirituality."

Cokesbury

Religious   1661 N. Northwest Hwy.
                                              Park Ridge, IL 60068
                                              708-299-4411
                                              Hours: Mon.-Fri. 9-5; Sat. 9-3

In business for over a century, Cokesbury stocks 40,000 titles devoted to religious studies. They will order any book in print but not in stock. However, chances are good that you'll find just what you're looking for in their stock. Cokesbury offers greeting cards, jewelry, church supplies, choir and clergy robes, altarware, and church signs. Twenty percent discounts are extended to the clergy and libraries.

Located on the first floor, the store is wheelchair accessible. With great concern, Nancy Barak, manager, points out that wheelchairers have to be able to jump a street curb after parking their car because sidewalks do not have smooth ramps to the street. Mass transit is available.

Cole's the Book People

General

604 Stratford Square Mall
Bloomingdale, IL 60108
708-893-7573
Hours: Mon.-Fri. 10-9;
Sat. 10-6; Sun. 11-5

Located in Stratford Square Mall of Bloomingdale, Cole's the Book People carries a large stock of general interest books. As a division of Waldenbooks, they are able to take advantage of their combined bookselling expertise which makes this bookstore a terrific place to visit when you need a break from mall shopping.

A Preferred Reader's Card enables you to a discount. Employees are happy to make recommendations which is a feature that customers really appreciate. Open everyday with plenty of parking nearby, Cole's the Book People is wheelchair accessible. If you are in the area, stop by and check out all that Cole's and the mall have to offer.

Coopersmith's

General

Woodfield Mall
Schaumburg, IL 60173
708-619-6850
Hours: Mon.-Fri. 10am-9;
Sat. 10-6; Sun. 11-6

The outside look of Coopersmith's bookstore in Woodfield Mall in Schaumburg is so inviting that one can't help but enter. Painted in hunter green and trimmed with gold, the front has a paned window which gives you the feel of an old fashioned bookstore. Once you enter, you're drawn to it's comfortable atmosphere and it's organized layout. It's easy to find the section you're looking for, but if you don't see what you're looking for, the employees are friendly and ready to help you when you ask them questions. It's a full service bookstore that will order any book not included in its stock of more than 30,000 titles. Gift wrapping is a free service.

So much for ambiance, now down to quality. At Coopersmith's, it's superb. Of particular interest are their departments of business, fiction, history, and biography. The selections are thorough and the complete works of many authors are available. Many of the books are beautifully bound and perfect for the coffee table. The children's section is outstanding. Among the other items offered are magazines, Mount Blanc pens, day planners, blank books, greeting cards, and small items perfect for gift giving.

This store is the largest of the three branches of Coopersmith's in the Chicago area. The other two are in Vernon Hills and on North Michigan Avenue in Chicago.

Coopersmith's in Woodfield Mall is wheelchair accessible and is located on the first floor. Coopersmith's is a delightful store to browse through and to choose those books destined for your home library.

Crown Books

General
28 E. Rand Rd.
Arlington Hts., IL 60004
708-577-1003
Hours: Mon.-Fri. 10-9;
Sat. 10-6; Sun. 11-5

Crown Books

General
1148 Lake Cook Road
Buffalo Grove, IL 60090
708-459-5717
Hours: Mon.-Fri. 10-9;
Sat. 10-6; Sun. 11-5

Crown Books

General
315 S. Rand Rd.
Lake Zurich, IL 60047
708-438-6166
Hours: Mon.-Fri. 10-9;
Sat. 10-6; Sun. 11-5

Crown Books

General
1016 S. Elmhurst Rd.
Mount Prospect, IL 60056
708-439-1180
Hours: Mon.-Fri. 10-9;
Sat. 10-6; Sun. 11-5

Crown Books

General   1400 E. Golf Rd.
                             Rolling Meadows, IL 60008
                             708-952-1200
                             <u>Hours:</u> Mon.-Fri. 10-9;
                             Sat. 10-6; Sun. 11-5

Crown Books

General   770 D Rollings Rd.
                             Round Lake Bch., IL 60073
                             708-740-2211
                             <u>Hours:</u> Mon.-Fri. 10-9;
                             Sat. 10-6; Sun. 11-5

Crown Books

General   862 W. Main St.
                             West Dundee, IL 60118
                             708-426-1160
                             <u>Hours:</u> Mon.-Fri. 10-9;
                             Sat. 10-6; Sun. 11-5

Doubleday Book Shop

General   Woodfield Mall
                             Schaumburg, IL 60173
                             708-330-1514
                             <u>Hours:</u> Mon.-Fri. 10-9;
                             Sat. 10-6; Sun. 11-5

Although the Doubleday Bookstore appears to be a small store in Woodfield Mall, they carry a large volume of books and are big on customer support. The store itself is comfortable for browsing and when a question is asked of an employee, the response is both helpful and friendly. They do special orders and free gift wrapping when requested.

At Doubleday, other businesses are very important clients. Doubleday often sells large quantities of books to businesses and extends them a special discount.

A local library has chosen Doubleday Bookstore as their bookstore of choice for purchasing Doubleday gift certificates as awards and prizes.

The books you'll find at Doubleday are all new and of a general interest nature. Particularly strong departments are business, psychology, history, fiction, cookbooks, and children's books. Doubleday Bookstore in Woodfield Mall is wheelchair accessible.

Drummer & Thumbs Bookstore

General

One East Campbell St.
Arlington Hts., IL 60005
708-398-8968
Hours: Mon.-Sat. 9-5;
Unannounced evening hours

"I love when someone calls or comes in and says: 'I've been looking everywhere for this book' and I can walk over to the shelf and pull it down," said Rob Baker. He and his mother Sheila say that they stock over 30,000 new and used books in this delightful bookstore. Many of the books are collector editions.

Topics are of general interest and most are top quality and of an eclectic orientation. On sunny summer days you may find two racks of books outside the store tempting you to enter.

Rob reports that they are currently computerizing, expanding their mail order business and expanding the children's book section. They recently obtained a toll-free phone number (800-696-9878). Often they are able to receive special order books in only three or four days. Drummer & Thumbs also does out-of-print book searches.

A variety of book accessories are available such as book lights, mylar book covers, bookmarks, bookplates, and, the ever-popular Cliff Notes.

Located in the heart of Arlington Heights very close to the CNW, Drummer & Thumbs Bookstore occupies a corner spot in the quaint downtown of this suburban town. Unfortunately it is not wheelchair accessible.

If you think all Drummer & Thumbs has to offer are books and book paraphernalia, you're wrong. Rob claims they offer special programs to requesting clients: "amateur psychology and counseling, friendly conversations and illuminating insights."

You must experience Drummer & Thumbs. It's a great place to visit and one you'll return to often.

Earthen Vessels Ltd.

Religious

43 S. Vail Ave.
Arlington Hts., IL 60005
708-398-2250
Hours: Mon. & Thurs. 9:30-8;
Tues., Wed., Fri., Sat. 9:30-5

Earthen Vessels Ltd. of suburban Arlington Heights is a Christian bookstore that carries books, Bibles, greeting cards, gifts for all occasions, Christian cassette tapes and compact disks. In 1992 they'll celebrate their tenth anniversary as a Christian bookstore.

Children are important people at Earthen Vessels. They offer a special selection of children's books and sponsor children's story telling sessions. For adults and children, author autographing sessions are a delightful way to meet your favorite Christian author.

The store is wheelchair accessible and both parking and mass transit are available. For the convenience of patrons, Earthen Vessels Ltd. has in-store seating and restrooms that are wheelchair accessible. Discounts are offered to churches. Special orders are welcome. They carry approximately 16,000 titles in stock.

Encyclopaedia Britannica Retail Store

Reference

Woodfield Mall
Schaumburg, IL 60173
708-347-7942
Hours: Mon.-Fri. 10-9;
Sat. 10-6; Sun. 11-5

The old traveling encyclopedia salesman is a relic but you can still take advantage of his wares. The Encyclopaedia Britannica Retail Store was scheduled to open in the Fall of 1991. This will be Encyclopaedia Britannica's pilot retail store and represents a new phase in the life of one of Chicago's most respected enterprises.

You'll be able to purchase more than your old favorite encyclopedia in this new store. You'll find history, geography, social sciences, literature, children's books, science, games, biographies, and, of course, reference. Having facts at your fingertips is a must today. The publishing business is responding by increasing the number of reference books in print and improving the aesthetic value of the books. This new retail store stocks well over 1,000 different reference titles.

The dear old Encyclopaedia Britannica is available in eight foreign languages. But there's so much more here: maps, globes, atlases, and video cassettes.

An exciting part of the new store is their computer software section. For sale will be Britannica Software's 25 floppy disk titles and over a dozen CD-ROM titles. The store will have six working personal computer stations so that customers can sample the learning software.

The company is planning for the store to be a multi-media learning center for the entire family. Cost of items range from $5 to $2,000. Customers will be able to join a Preferred Shopper Club and receive discounts. They also will offer a guest registry.

Remaining true to their dedication to customers, the store will publish its own newsletter to keep patrons informed of the special events taking place in the store. They plan to sponsor author autographing sessions, and a variety of demonstrations.

The store will be completely wheelchair accessible within Woodfield Mall and will total 1,700 square feet in size.

Encyclopaedia Britannica Retail Store will be a must for everyone. In today's world, we all need to broaden our horizons and this store adds fun to learning.

Family Bookstore

Religious   Woodfield Mall, Space D315
                                               Schaumburg, IL 60173
                                               708-240-2410
                                               <u>Hours:</u> Mon.-Fri. 10-9; Sat. 10-6

Please refer to the description of the Family Bookstore listed in the Western Suburbs chapter of *The Book Lover's Guide.*

Family Bookstore

Religious   Westview Center
                                               Streamwood, IL 60107
                                               708-483-0269
                                               <u>Hours:</u> Mon.-Fri. 10-9; Sat. 10-6

Please refer to the description of the Family Bookstore listed in the Western Suburbs chapter of *The Book Lover's Guide.*

Heartland Books

General

214 Main Street
Woodstock, IL 60098
815-338-5272
Hours: Mon.-Sat. 11-5;
Sun. 12-5

Owners of Heartland Books in suburban Woodstock, Anthony and Lydia Medici, call themselves "avid readers and all-around book nuts." They have created a bookstore to please the like-minded.

Dealing with used, out-of-print and antique books they stock 15,000 titles. They have rounded-up an extensive selection of books that focus on the American West: cowboys, outlaws, Indians, frontier military, mountain men, and even Western art and artists. Another specialty section deals with hunting, fishing and guns.

Heartland Books also stocks good quality used books emphasizing modern and classic literature, American, English and foreign history, mystery (heavy on the English mystery), art, architecture, and an engaging potpourri of books in other fields. It's easy to spend hours browsing the tall shelves and sinking into easy chairs while making decisions.

The store is completely wheelchair accessible. Parking and mass transit are nearby.

"Woodstock is a lovely old town," Lydia reports. "It's historic square, with the famous Woodstock Opera House, County Jail and Court House is worth a trip alone."

The Chicago Northwestern Railroad pulls into the Woodstock Station only one block from Heartland Books. Good restaurants and antique stores in the area are abundant. Heartland Books is located in the Merchants Antique Row building. If you're traveling by car, take the Northwest Tollway to Route 47, go North and you'll find the small town of Woodstock.

Call Anthony and Lydia to find out when they will next hold a book appraisal session. You can discover treasures within your personal library.

Hooked on History

History

Antiques Center
100 W. Northwest Highway
Mt. Prospect, IL 60056
708-255-2340
Hours: Everyday 10-5

"I am a specialist in American history," said Bruce Herrick of Hooked on History. He notes that his specialties include the Civil War,

Western Americana, American Revolution, World War II, and American Presidents.

In addition to 5,000 used and antiquarian books, Hooked on History carries Civil War newspapers and prints. Bruce participates in 15-20 Civil War and antiquarian book shows each year. A search service is available and Bruce is interested in buying your historical collections.

The Antiques Center location is in a large building that is stuffed with antique delights. Stores are not set up like a traditional business with a storefront. Instead, businesses operate in sections. This makes the entire place appear to be a large antique flee market. You can either enjoy weaving in and out of displays and search for Hooked on History's area or you can ask the many friendly workers at the Antique Center.

The center is wheelchair accessible but some little nooks and crannies are too narrow to maneuver through. Parking is close by and mass transit is available.

If you're looking for an adventure in book hunting, you must visit Hooked on History. Scattered throughout the Antiques Center, you'll find old books filtered in between antique cut glass and sparkling jewels.

Irish Boutique

Irish

434 Coffin Road
Long Grove, IL 60047
708-634-3540
Hours: Mon.-Sat. 10-5;
Sun. 11-5

An Irish man or woman knows that "Cead Mile Failte" means one hundred thousand welcomes and that's just what you'll receive at the Irish Boutique in the quaint little shopping area of Long Grove. Because of the great demand for Irish products, the Irish Boutique has expanded to three shops. Fortunately the store that houses the books is wheelchair accessible.

Books published in Ireland and America are for sale. The collection of approximately 700 books includes Irish history, fiction, heraldry, humor, children's, travel, cooking, and classic literature. A great number of books are about Ireland's political situation in the north, both past and present. They also have an impressive selection of books about Irish genealogy including passenger lists on ships sailing to America in the 1800's.

The Irish Boutique also sells popular and traditional Irish music on tape cassettes and compact discs. So that you can sample the music for sale, they play the music throughout the store. Of course, they also sell a wonderful selection of Irish gifts from coffee mugs to crystal to clothing. If it's Irish, the Irish Boutique is bound to have just the item you're looking for.

Jack's Used Books

Used   718 E. Northwest Hwy.
                                          Mt. Prospect, IL 60056
                                          708-398-7767
                                          Hours: Mon.-Fri. 9-5;
                                          Thurs. 9-9; Sat. 9:30-4

Jack's Used Books has one of the largest inventories of used books in Chicagoland. Located in a mini-mall in suburban Mount Prospect, Jack's is reasonably organized considering the large number of books coming and going daily. The stock usually totals 30,000 titles, half of which are hardbacks, half are paperback. Most are of mass market interest and range from top quality collector items to mass-market paperbacks.

With terribly close aisles, the store is difficult for wheelchairs. Off-street parking is available and the CNW station is a few blocks away.

Kroch's & Brentano's Inc.

General   708 W. Northwest Highway
                                          Barrington, IL 60010
                                          708-304-4020
                                          Hours: Mon.- Wed., Fri. 10-6;
                                          Thurs. 10-8; Sat. 10-5:30;
                                          Sun. noon-5

Kroch's & Brentano's Inc.

General   999 Elmhurst Road
                                          Mt. Prospect, IL 60056
                                          708-259-5510
                                          Hours: Mon.-Fri. 10-9;
                                          Sat. 10-6; Sun. 11-5

Lemstone Books

Religious

1190 Spring Hill Mall
West Dundee, IL 60118
708-426-9355
Hours: Mon.-Fri. 10-9;
Sat. 10-6; Sun. 11-5

Logos of Park Ridge

Religious

134 S. Euclid Ave.
Park Ridge, IL 60068
708-696-4090
Hours: Mon.-Wed, Fri. 10-6;
Thurs. 10-8; Sat. 9:30-5

Lose's Book Nook

General

81 Market
Elgin, IL 60120
708-468-1422
Hours: Mon.-Fri. 10-6; Sat. 9-4

"We are the only bookstore that we know of in Northern Illinois that offers a credit exchange program for hardcovers and children's books as well as the paperbacks," stated Glen Lose, owner of Lose's Book Nook in suburban Elgin. Glen also boasts that his is the only full service bookstore in Elgin.

In addition to offering 11,900 books, Glen offers his customers special events. At different times you can find patrons enjoying live music and children's story telling. A newsletter keeps his patrons informed of events. He also will search for specific books when requested.

Prices are of concern to customers and Glen offers terrific discounts: 1/2 price used paperbacks, 1/2 price or less for used hardcovers, and new paperbacks and hardcovers discounted from 10-20%. Topics are of interest to the general reader with special attention to children's books.

Lose's Book Nook is on three levels and the lower level is totally devoted to children's and young adult's books. The store is wheelchair accessible but the levels inside make it difficult to maneuver. Also for sale you'll find artwork and oil paintings.

Marshall Field & Co. Book Dept.

General   Woodfield Mall
                                   Schaumburg, IL 60173
                                   708-619-1234
                                   Hours: Mon.-Fri. 10-9;
                                   Sat. 10-6; Sun. 11-5

The Olive Branch, Ltd.

Religious   11 E. Northwest Hwy
                                   Palatine, IL 60067
                                   708-991-3966
                                   Hours: Mon. Thurs. 9-8;
                                   Tues., Wed., Fri. 9-6; Sat. 9-5

A Christian book and gift shop, The Olive Branch carries many categories of books including arts & crafts, biography, education, psychology, social sciences, fine art, fiction, philosophy, women's studies, music, children's books and, of course, religion. With the special needs of some customers in mind, The Olive Branch also sells audio books and large type print books. Titles in stock reach 2,000.

"We provide a place of serene, caring atmosphere," said Helen Moffett, Vice President of The Olive Branch.

With Christian music playing in the store, the customer will find gifts, cards, wall hangings, video and cassette music tapes. Bring your kids--The Olive Branch has a play corner with children's books.

The store is wheelchair accessible and has off-street parking nearby. Inside the store, you'll find chairs to rest as you make your selections.

Paperback Paperback

Used   131 S. Northwest Hwy.
                                   Park Ridge, IL 60068
                                   708-698-0131
                                   Hours: Mon.-Fri. 10-5:30;
                                   Sat. 10-4:30

When you're in the mood for a good mystery, romance, or science fiction book, check out Paperback Paperback. (They liked it so much, they named it twice. Sorry, old joke.)

At Paperback Paperback you'll find 8-10,000 new and used books. A trade-in discount system enables you to read your favorite books at reduced prices. Also in stock are current magazines and they will special order hardbacks.

The store is wheelchair accessible.

Plain Tales Books

Antiquarian

Box 1691
Arlington Hts., IL 60006
708-253-1472
Hours: Mail order only

Owner of Plain Tales Books in Arlington Heights, Thomas Zimmerman sells and buys used books of quality. The business operates on a mail order basis.

His collection for sale includes modern first editions, general out-of-print books with topics covering literature, travel and tourism, and a special selection about India. Currently there are over 2,000 titles in stock. The business began operations in 1985.

If you are a collector, write to Plain Tales Books for a catalogue.

Reader's Haven Paperback Book Exchange

Used

815 Saint Charles St.
Elgin, IL 60120
708-697-2526
Hours: Tues.-Fri. 10-6; Sat. 10-5

If you like romances and hunting for great book deals, head out to the Reader's Haven Paperback Book Exchange in Elgin. Robert Donholm, owner, is such an expert in managing a thriving new/used bookstore, he gave an hour lecture at the 1990 Romantic Times National Convention in San Antonio, Texas.

With many price discounts, customer pocketbooks are always happy at Reader's Haven. All new paperbacks are discounted 10% on a cash only basis. The real deals start when you make your selections from the used racks. Used books sell for savings from 50% to 75% off the original cost of the book. You can bring your old paperbacks, trade them in, and receive a credit of 20% of the original cost of the book. The credit can be applied toward purchase of used books. As an extra bonus, if your cash purchase totals $15.00 or more, you can have a free used book of your choice.

Bob reports that the store sells 2-3,000 books per week. What is amazing is that in spite of this high volume, the store is categorized and, in most cases, filed alphabetically by author. This time-consuming filing system makes it easy for customers to locate books they want in a timely manner. Three categories abound: romance, fiction, and mystery. Established in 1976 around the same time of the romance book-boom, Reader's Haven continues specializing in this genre. Owner Bob says that he's surprised that men are beginning to choose romances as their reading choice and many new authors in the field are men.

Customers can also enjoy author autographing sessions which are held 4-5 times per year. Finger foods, punch, coffee, and lots of book chatter fill the store. The Reader's Haven Paperback Book Exchange has been in "Romantic Times" magazine five times. The store always participates in the annual "Book Lovers Day" celebration which features romance writers, new and old.

Parking and mass transit are available but the store is not wheelchair accessible from the outside. There are two steps into the store which is do-able for strollers. Inside, the store is wheelchair accessible.

Stop by Reader's Haven and be sure to talk with Bob. You'll benefit from his expertise in the romance book field. Follow his recommendations and you'll always be pleased with your choices.

Salvation Army Book Dept.

Religion

10 W. Algonquin
Des Plaines, IL 60616
708-803-3400
Hours: Call

When you think of the Salvation Army, you probably don't think of their book department. You should. They have a large book department covering religious and music topics. Musical compact discs and cassettes for adults and children are available as well as a variety of gifts including Precious Moments.

Recently relocated to their new site in Des Plaines, mail order represents 85 percent of their business.

Sandpiper Books Inc.

Used

185 E. Lake
Bloomingdale, IL 60108
708-980-3199
Hours: Mon.-Fri. 10-6;
Sat. 10-5

Looking for a place to find used paperbacks in the far northwestern suburbs? Try Sandpiper Books Inc. in Bloomingdale. You'll find over 25,000 books in your favorite categories: romances (both historical and gothic), science fiction, horror, mystery, and books for the kids. As a added bonus, they also sell new and used comic books.

There is one step into the store but otherwise it is wheelchair accessible. Sandpiper Books is located in Circle Center shopping area.

School of Metaphysics Bookstore

Metaphysics

222 W. Wilson
Palatine, IL 60067
708-991-0140
Hours: Appointment only

"My mission is to light the fire for people," says Bev Lauer, Director. "Then I keep the tinder going by supplying people with the tools they need to learn how to live."

Open to the general public and students of the School of Metaphysics, the bookstore carries approximately 300 titles focusing on metaphysics. Headquarters are in Missouri and there are eighteen schools across the United States. The school located in Palatine is the largest.

The philosophy of the school is, according to Bev: "To aid any individual who is willing to put forth the effort to become a whole functioning self - not dependent upon any individual or thing for their peace, security, or contentment."

The faculty often speaks at meetings, conventions, and seminars on topics such as Take This Job, and Love It; SoulMates; Dreams: Your Subconscious Connection; Mind: The Final Frontier; Positive Thinking in a Negative World; Past Lives, and Present Memories. After extensive study, some students go on to be teachers.

During private readings, you can find out things about yourself you probably didn't know, such as Past Life, Past Life Crossings (about you and another individual), Time of Birth; Health Analysis; Business Analysis, and Family Readings.

"Students come from all walks of life. Everyone who studies is learning how to live life to the fullest," Bev added.

In operation since 1973, the School of Metaphysics has served thousands of people from all walks of life. Adult evening classes meet one night per week and correspondence courses are available. The school is a not-for-profit educational and service organization that is supported by donations. Currently, they are located in a home where there are stairs, making it difficult for wheelchairs.

Open your mind and visit the School of Metaphysics Bookstore. You may find a part of yourself that you didn't know existed.

Sidney Johnson Bookseller

General

119 E. Main St.
Barrington, IL 60010
708-381-0084
Hours: Mon.-Sat. 9-5:30

"We bring books and people together to make a terrific combination," says Sidney Johnson who operates a beautiful 2,000 square foot bookstore in Barrington. The bookstore sells new general interest books with an emphasis on fine art and children's books.

Good service is a top priority here. Sidney notes long associations with clients and still receives calls from customers who have moved out-of-state. She says she will "do whatever it takes to please a customer." Special orders are no problem.

Established in 1975, the store is, unfortunately, not wheelchair accessible.

Victor Kahn, Medical Book Consultant

Medical

211 W. Emerson St.
Arlington Hts., IL 60005
708-437-1417
Hours: Mail order only

Professionals within the medical world often do not have the time to shop for medical books. Victor Kahn is the man to turn to for medical books. He works exclusively by phone and mail order.

Victor Kahn is an excellent resource for physicians, dentists, veterinarians, hospitals, and medical libraries. All of the books he works with must be special-ordered and are not in stock on his shelves.

Waldenbooks

General

445 E. Palatine Road
Arlington Hts., IL 60004
708-259-1340
Hours: Mon.-Fri. 10-9;
Sat. 10-6; Sun. 11-5

Waldenbooks

General

Woodfield Mall
Schaumburg, IL 60173
708-619-6850
Hours: Mon.-Fri. 10-9;
Sat. 10-6; Sun. 11-5

Waldenkids

Children's

1006 Spring Hill Mall
West Dundee, IL 60118
708-428-6319
Hours: Mon.-Fri. 10-9;
Sat. 10-6; Sun. 11-5

Williams-Sonoma

Cooking, Nutrition

Woodfield Mall
Schaumburg, IL 60173
708-619-0940
Hours: Mon.-Fri. 10-9;
Sat. 10-6; Sun. 11-5

The Williams-Sonoma name should make your taste buds tingle.
They specialize in gourmet cooking and have the books and cookware to
achieve any wizardry you can create in your kitchen.

Southern Suburbs

Andrews & Rose Booksellers

Used

Antique Mall 2423 S. 11th
Niles, MI 49120
616-684-7001
Hours: Everyday 10-6

Andrews & Rose Booksellers

Used

105 East Main Street
Niles, MI 49120
616-683-4251
Hours: Mon.-Sat. noon-5

The objective of Andrews & Rose Booksellers is to offer unusual used and out-of-print books in excellent condition on all subjects. They achieve their objective by stocking 10,000 quality used books.

They have two stores both located in Niles, Michigan that each carry thousands of selections. The main store is located at 105 East Main Street and is open Monday through Saturday from noon until 5:00 p.m. The subsidiary outlet in the Antique Mall at 2423 South Eleventh Street is open daily from 10:00 a.m. until 6:00 p.m.

If you are looking for a nice afternoon drive and enjoy browsing through books, point your car in the direction of Andrews & Rose bookstores.

B. Dalton Bookseller

General

711 Chicago Ridge Mall
Chicago Ridge, IL 60415
708-636-0397
<u>Hours:</u> Mon.-Fri. 10-9;
Sat. 10-5:30; Sun. 11-5

B. Dalton Bookseller

General

109 Lincoln Mall
Matteson, IL 60443
708-481-7272
<u>Hours:</u> Mon.-Sat. 10-9;
Sun. 11-5

B. Dalton Bookseller

General

115 Center of Park Forest
Park Forest, IL 60466
708-747-4072
<u>Hours:</u> Mon.-Fri. 10-9;
Sat. 10-5:30; Sun. 11-5

Bible Book Center

Religious

3847 W. 95th St.
Evergreen Park, IL 60642
708-422-7060
<u>Hours:</u> Mon.-Wed. 9-5:30;
Thurs., Fri. 9-8; Sat. 9-5:30

Stocking books for all denominations, the Bible Book Center specializes in selling Bibles with some written in Spanish. As a service, they do imprinting on Bibles.

In addition to religious books, the Bible Book Center sells greeting cards, wedding gifts, and church supplies. The store is not wheelchair accessible.

Bits & Pieces of History

Civil War

8707 S. Meade
Burbank, IL 60459
708-423-5966
Hours: Mon.-Sat. 1pm-4pm;
Appointments; mail order

When you are scanning Bits & Pieces of History, you may notice that many of the old photographs are strangely familiar. It's not surprising. The authors of the Time Life book series about the Civil War found many of the photos they used at Bits & Pieces of History. Many authors writing about the late 1800's conduct research at this store.

The books available are out-of-print and of antiquarian quality. In addition to stocking books about the Civil War, western expansion, American Indians, and American biographies, you'll discover a vast range of documents, artifacts, bonds, and photographs.

The business basically operates by mail order and by appointment. The store is often represented at various book fairs.

The Book Inn

Used

508 W. Washington St.
South Bend, IN 46601
219-288-1990
Hours: Bed & Breakfast

Many of us use a book to abstract ourselves from life's day to day pressures, but find that the outside world still intrudes. We need to get physically away and The Book Inn is the perfect hideaway that you need.

Located in South Bend, Indiana, you can check into a beautiful 1872 French Victorian Bed and Breakfast, browse through their 6,000 quality used books, make your purchase, and retire to your room to relax.

The book selection is mostly non-fiction with a smattering of classics, detective fiction, cookbooks and children's favorites. Quality books are bought and sold.

The stately home was originally built by Albert Cushing, a local businessman who operated a book store. The decorative front entry reportedly won first place for design at the 1893 Columbian Exposition in Chicago. Today, the house is listed by the Indiana Historic Site Preservation Committee as an outstanding example of Second Empire architecture. In May, 1991 the house was honored by the Women's Association of the South Bend Symphony Orchestra as the Designer's Showcase.

Each of the five guest rooms have private bathrooms and air conditioning combining the beauty of the past with the comforts of today.

Rooms are appropriately named and each has it's special flavor. "The Louisa May Alcott Room" has a cozy reading nook, "The Cushing Suite" features a spacious bay window, "The Jane Austen Room" has a beautiful view of the lavish grounds, "The Charlotte Bronte Room" has a quiet desk cove, and "The Jesse Willcox Smith Suite" is light and airy.

Unfortunately for wheelchair users, the Book Inn has twelve steps to the front door. Because the home is a part of the Southold Historic Group, no alterations can be made to accomodate handicap access.

Remember the Book Inn for a close get-away. The coffee pot is always brewing and ready for you.

Calvary Bookstore

Religious

16125 S. Park Ave.
South Holland, IL 60473
708-333-1115
Hours: Mon.-Thurs. 9:30-5:30;
Fri. 9:30-8; Sat. 9:30-5

As you stroll in the Calvary Bookstore, don't forget to listen to the music playing. If you like the music, you can purchase a cassette tape in the store.

With a focus on religious books, the Calvary Bookstore also offers children's books and fiction. You will be able to purchase figurines, pictures, plaques, greeting cards, wedding candles, gift wrapping and miscellaneous small items. The store will imprint Bibles to your specifications, gift wrap the Bible, and even mail it wherever you would like. Occasionally, authors visit and autograph their books. Special discount sales and coupons are available to specific times.

The store has no stairs and it is easy for a wheelchair to get into the store but aisles are too tight to maneuver within the store.

Christian Literature Center

Religious

2340 177th St.
Lansing, IL 60438
708-895-0005
Hours: Mon.-Wed., Fri.
9:30-5:30; Thurs. 9:30-8;
Sat. 9:30-5

In stock at Christian Literature Center are over 2,000 Christian books, video and music tapes, pictures, T-shirts, posters, greeting cards, and trinkets and toys for children. Some books are printed in large print or Spanish. The store is wheelchair accessible.

150

Crown Books

General

592 River Oaks West
Calumet City, IL 60409
708-868-1144
Hours: Mon.-Fri. 10-9;
Sat. 10-6; Sun. 11-5

Crown Books

General

242 Commons Dr.
Chicago Ridge, IL 60415
708-424-4944
Hours: Mon.-Fri. 10-9;
Sat. 10-6; Sun. 11-5

Crown Books

General

17840 S. Halsted St.
Homewood, IL 60430
708-799-0334
Hours: Mon.-Fri. 10-8;
Sat. 10-6; Sun. 11-5

Crown Books

General

154 Town Center
Matteson, IL 60443
708-747-4222
Hours: Mon.-Fri. 10-9;
Sat. 10-6; Sun. 11-5

Crown Books

General

8722 S. Cicero Ave.
Oak Lawn, IL 60453
708-499-1313
Hours: Mon.-Fri. 10-9;
Sat. 10-6; Sun. 11-5

Crown Books

General

15014 La Grange Rd.
Orland Park, IL 60462
708-460-4840
Hours: Mon.-Fri. 10-9;
Sat. 10-6; Sun. 11-5

Exchange-A-Book

Used

1507 Burnham Ave.
Calumet City, IL 60409
708-862-9797
Hours: Mon.-Sat. 9-7

Nancy McCann, owner of Exchange-A-Book bookstore, is a very busy lady. She says she's careful about discussing her ideas out loud because they all seem to come true. Nancy doesn't have small ideas. Her book stock includes 200,000 titles.

In addition to managing the bookstore, she supports a writing group that meets weekly, publishes a monthly magazine, and conducts an annual author's convention. For four years, Nancy sponsored a public access television program where authors could talk about writing.

Exchange-A-Book is interested in both their customers (who buy and sell new and used books) and writers. In 1983 Nancy helped a writer's group of pre-published romance writers. Today, the group has evolved into members who specialize in most forms of writing.

To further support writers, Exchange-A-Book holds a writer's conference each fall. In October, 1991, they will conduct their ninth conference. Approximately 270 people attend the conference. At the conference in 1991 a special Author's Auction was held. Many authors donated items that were auctioned with funds given to the Illinois Literacy Council. Publishing company editors and literary agents conduct workshops that people can attend.

Exchange-A-Book goes one step further: they publish a review magazine titled "Rendezvous" which is in its eighth year of publication. Published monthly, the magazine is filled with book reviews written by the writers group associated with the store. Publishers including Pocket, Avon, Bantam, Signet, Harlequin and Silhouette send review copies of their books before the book is released to the general public. This enables the Exchange-A-Book group to read the book and write the review which appears in the "Rendezvous" magazine at the same time the book is released for sale to the general public.

Members of Exchange-A-Book writer's group speak at libraries and clubs upon request. Meeting weekly, the group discusses pieces that members have written or critique the work of other writers. About 25 people are members, many of whom have been with the group since it started in 1983.

Family owned and operated since 1980, Exchange-A-Book sell new and used books of all types of paperbacks. Their 2,400 square feet hold an ever changing number of selections, usually around 200,000 volumes. Illinois State Lottery tickets are also for sale. Many of the new books stocked are discounted. Services available include a mail order service and special ordering books.

The store is wheelchair accessible but Nancy notes that often aisles are crowded. "But," she adds, "we are glad to help the disabled." Employees are well informed and very friendly.

Nancy will be a member of a forum of publishers, distributors, and booksellers at the upcoming fourth National Romance Writers of America Conference. She attends all of the conventions sponsored by Romantic Times national magazine.

Exchange-A-Book is a fine bookstore to visit and Nancy is one energetic, enthusiastic lady. Stop by this store and you may become a part of a dream that you have. Nancy seems to make her wishes come true.

Family Bookstore

Religious   236 Lincoln Mall
                                               Matteson, IL 60443
                                               708-748-8845
                                               Hours: Mon.-Sat. 10-9

The Family Bookstore located in Matteson sells over 1,000 Christian books including fiction and Bibles. Also for sale are music compact discs and cassettes, pictures, and wall hangings. Of special interest are beautiful book covers to protect that special book.

The store is wheelchair accessible.

Family Bookstore

Religious   156 Orland Square Mall
                                               Orland Park, IL 60562
                                               708-403-1998
                                               Hours: Mon.-Fri. 10-9; Sat. 10-6

Please refer to the description of the Family Bookstore listed in the Western Suburbs chapter of *The Book Lover's Guide*.

Katzy Book Shop

General

3512 Ridge Rd.
Lansing, IL 60438
708-474-0293
Hours: Mon.-Wed., Fri. 10-6;
Thurs. 10-8; Sat. 10-5

"We strive not to just make a sale but to sell the right book to the right person," Judith J. Bobalik, owner of Katzy Book Shop said. As a unique offer, the book shop gives patrons a 10% discount during the month of his/her birthday. Everyone is welcome to take part in the book shop's frequent buyer card which allows a discounted price on the 14th book after purchasing 13 books.

Located in Lansing, Illinois, Katzy Book Shop sells 4,000+ new books including cookery, mystery, and children's books. In addition, they offer greeting cards, bookmarks, and a few puzzles and games. Other services available are gift wrapping, mailing, and gift certificates. At times, they sponsor author autograph sessions.

Katzy Book Shop is wheelchair accessible and seating is available while you shop. On street parking and mass transit are close.

Kroch's & Brentano's Inc.

General

18 River Oaks Center
Calumet City, IL 60409
708-868-1666
Hours: Mon.-Fri. 10-9;
Sat. 10-6; Sun. 11-5

Kroch's & Brentano's Inc.

General

J-6 Evergreen Plaza
Evergreen Park, IL 60642
708-424-9550
Hours: Mon.-Fri. 10-9;
Sat. 10-6; Sun. 11-5

Kroch's & Brentano's Inc.

General

159 Lincoln Mall
Matteson, IL 60443
708-481-6140
Hours: Mon.-Sat. 10-9;
Sun. 11-5

Kroch's & Brentano's Inc.

General

100 Orland Square
151st & Rt. 45
Orland Park, IL 60462
708-349-0676
Hours: Mon.-Fri. 10-9;
Sat. 10-6; Sun. 11-5

Lemstone Books

Religious

641 Chicago Ridge Mall
Chicago Ridge, IL 60415
708-425-7373
Hours: Mon.-Fri. 10-9;
Sat. 10-5:30; Sun. 11-5

Little Professor Book Center

General

Lakeview Plaza, 15838
LaGrange Rd.
Orland Park, IL 60462
708-403-7711
Hours: Mon.-Fri. 10-9;
Sat. 11-6; Sun. noon-5

Little Professor Book Centers are a fast growing chain in the Chicago area. One establishment is found in the Lakeview Plaza in Orland Park. Open daily, they stock more than 5,000 titles of general interest books.

Topics include business, management, psychology, literature, magic, philosophy, health, nutrition, children's books, audio books, and magazines. Non-book items for sale are book ends, book marks, book lights, puppets, and audio cassette tapes. Free gift wrapping is only one service they offer. They also sponsor a bonus book club and accept orders by telephone.

The store is wheelchair accessible.

Pyramid Book Mart Inc.

Metaphysics

3580 W. 95th St.
Evergreen Park, IL 60642
708-636-2233
Hours: Tues.-Sat. 10-5;
Thurs. 10-7

A metaphysical book store, Pyramid Book Mart sells self-help books and audio tapes, quartz crystals and jewelry. The store has been in business for seven years and is wheelchair accessible.

Robert & Phyllis Weinberg Books

Mail order

15145 Oxford Dr.
Oak Forest, IL 60452
708-687-5765
Hours: Appointment only

The connoisseur of science fiction, fantasy, and horror must get his or her name on the mailing list of Robert & Phyllis Weinberg Books. In addition to a full stock of current editions, they also sell some rare and unusual books that are author autographed and limited editions.

Hard-to-find books are easy to find when you contact the Weinbergs. Names that a true fan will recognize that Robert & Phyllis have included in their stock are H.P. Lovecraft, Dean Koontz, Joe Landsdale, and F. Paul Wilson. They also have the complete line of Arkham House books. Many of the books they carry are published by small publishers.

Robert is a respected anthologist who has compiled fifty anthologies of science fiction, fantasy, and horror short stories. All of his anthologies are available through their catalogues.

If you're looking for the unique science fiction, fantasy, and horror books, look no further. Call to add your name to their mailing list. Sample catalogues are available for fifty cents.

Waldenbooks

General   Coles 410 Chicago Ridge Mall
                                            Chicago Ridge, IL 60415
                                            708-424-9190
                                            <u>Hours:</u> Mon.-Fri. 10-9;
                                            Sat. 11-5; Sun. noon-5:30

Waldenbooks

General   832 Orland Square
                                            Orland Park, IL 60462
                                            708-349-8823
                                            <u>Hours:</u> Mon.-Fri. 10-9;
                                            Sat. 11-6; Sun. 11-5

Western Suburbs

Anderson's Bookshop

General

5112 Main St.
Downers Grove, IL 60515
708-963-2665
Hours: Mon.-Fri. 9-9; Sat. 9-6
[winter: Sat. 9-5; Sun. 11-5]

Anderson's Bookshop in Downers Grove has been a favorite of many commuters catching the train across the street. Their general selection covers many tastes. Special orders are no problem. A big collection of newspapers, magazines, and greeting cards are available.

The children's section is located two steps above the rest of the store. In addition to books, they also stock book-related toys and play-mobiles.

Anderson's has two entrances, one in the front and another in the back of the store. The front entrance is wheelchair accessible as is the store except the children's section.

Anderson's Bookshop

General

176 N. York Rd.
Elmhurst, IL 60126
708-832-6566
Hours: Mon.-Fri. 9-9;
Sat. 9-6; Sun. 11-5

The newest of the three branches of Anderson's Bookshop is located in Elmhurst. Joining in the high quality tradition set by the Downers Grove and Naperville branches, the stock includes books for a broad interest range.

Children's books are also a specialty here and programs just for kids are conducted on Saturday's at 1:00 pm. The store's newsletter keeps you informed as to the type of program planned. They make an effort to offer special programs for different ages. For example, they've hosted a Dancing Bear story time for tots and a Babysitting Club meeting for the older child.

Author autographing sessions are periodically conducted in this, the largest of the three Anderson's Bookshops. The store is completely wheelchair accessible. Discounts up to 10% are given to those who belong to a special buyer's club.

Anderson's Bookshop

General

123 W. Jefferson
Naperville, IL 60540
708-355-2665
Hours: Mon.-Fri. 9-9;
Sat. 9-6; Sun. 11-5

Anderson's Bookshop in Naperville caters to children. When they hold their children's parties characters from children's literature often attend. Curious George and Clifford are favorites at the parties. Children's story telling is a delightful way to lead children to books. Educational toys are also available.

Anderson's hasn't forgotten the adults. They stock a variety of topics and feature mystery, travel and tourism, science fiction, and education. The staff are all book lovers and are happy to share opinions about books. They also sell greeting cards, gift wrap, and musical cassettes and compact discs. They will be happy to search for out-of-print books and mail your purchases for you.

Special programs they offer are a newsletter, author autographing sessions, and live in-store music. Bookcard members receive a 10% discount. When teachers make purchases for use in their classrooms, they receive a 20% discount.

The store is wheelchair accessible and off-street parking is available.

On your next outing with your children, be sure to take them to Anderson's Bookshop. You can enjoy browsing while the kids delight in their own section of books.

B. Dalton Bookseller

General

No. 417 Stratford Square Center
Bloomingdale, IL 60108
708-351-9559
Hours: Mon.-Fri. 10-9;
Sat. 10-6; Sun. 11-5

B. Dalton Bookseller

General

Yorktown Ctr.
Lombard, IL 60148
708-627-1484
<u>Hours:</u> Mon.-Fri. 10-9;
Sat. 10:30-5:30; Sun. 12-5

B. Dalton Bookseller

General

Iroquois Ctr., 1163 E. Ogden
Naperville, IL 60563
708-355-5263
<u>Hours:</u> Mon.-Fri. 10-9;
Sat. 10-5; Sun. 12-5

B. Dalton Bookseller

General

St. Charles Mall
St. Charles, IL 60174
708-584-6888
<u>Hours:</u> Mon.-Fri. 10-9;
Sat. 10-5; Sun. 11-5

B. Dalton Bookseller

General

The Courtyard
100-1 E. Roosevelt
Villa Park, IL 60181
708-832-0530
<u>Hours:</u> Mon.-Fri. 10-9;
Sat. 10-5; Sun. 12-5

B. Dalton Bookseller

General   Woodgrove Fes., 1000-75th St.
                                          Woodridge, IL 60517
                                          708-985-3383
                                          Hours: Mon.-Fri. 10-9;
                                          Sat. 10-5:30; Sun. 12-5

BOOKids

Children's   Fox Valley Mall
                                          Aurora, IL 60504

Scheduled to open in the Fall of 1991. A division of Lemstone Books.

Barbara's Bookstore

General   1110 Lake Street
                                          Oak Park, IL 60301
                                          708-848-9140
                                          Hours: Mon.-Sat. 10-10;
                                          Sun. 11-8

A popular bookstore located in suburban Oak Park (just north of the subway and CNW rail lines), this branch of Barbara's Bookstore stocks 27,000 different titles and has 68,000 books in stock. All areas of the store are wheelchair accessible except the children's section. This department is up three steps and is delightfully decorated with a huge storybook castle. They are currently expanding their recovery and self-help sections. This branch of Barbara's was established in 1975 and is only a few blocks away from several buildings designed by Frank Lloyd Wright. Barbara's is a "must-see" stop on any tour of Oak Park by a Book Lover.

See the full write-up describing all of the Barbara's Bookstores in the Chicago Central chapter of *The Book Lover's Guide to Chicagoland*.

The Book Rack

Used

1007A Ogden Ave.
Naperville, IL 60540
708-355-3505
<u>Hours:</u> Mon.-Fri. 10-5:30;
Sat. 10-4

The Book Rack

Used

1062 Hill Grove
Western Springs, IL 60558
708-246-2225
<u>Hours:</u> Mon.-Fri. 10-5:30;
Sat. 10-4

The Book Rack in Western Springs celebrated their sixteenth year in 1991. They sell popular used paperbacks and are always willing to discuss your trade-ins. The store is wheelchair accessible with assistance.

Books & Bytes Inc.

Computer

1163 E. Ogden, #105
Naperville, IL 60563
708-416-0163
<u>Hours:</u> Mon.-Fri. 9:30-9;
Sat. 10-6; Sun. 12-5

When personal computers gained popularity, another business started booming: books about computers. Chicagoland has it's own store that specializes in computer books, appropriately titled Books & Bytes. Established in 1987, Books and Bytes stocks over 3,500 titles about computers for the novice and expert.

Employees who know their business are able to assist and direct customers to the book meeting their needs. A programmer is always on duty to answer your tough questions. The friendly service is one of the specialties of the store. Naturally, they have a CD ROM (Compact Disk Read Only Memory) that permits rapid book searches. They will special order any book in print in the United States and ship it to you.

A newsletter keeps patrons up-to-date. The owners of the store are planning to start a book club. Often clubs and firms visit Books & Bytes to discuss the computing trade. In addition to the extensive book selection, Books & Bytes sells Prolog software, magazines, T-shirts and more. The store is wheelchair accessible.

Books By Choice

Religious   2711 Copperfield Dr.
                                              Naperville, IL 60565
                                              708-416-8758
                                              <u>Hours:</u> Mail Order

When your reading material of choice is Christian books, choose Books By Choice. Operated through mail order, Books By Choice conducts a mass mailing five times per year. The books on their lists are for pre-schoolers through eighth grade. Employees are familiar with the books and can make specific recommendations. Special orders are taken.

The Booksmith

Used   108 S. Marion
                                              Oak Park, IL 60302
                                              708-383-8734
                                              <u>Hours:</u> Tues.-Fri. 11-7;
                                              Sat. 10-4:30

More than 10,000 used books line the shelves at The Booksmith in Oak Park. They're all just waiting for you. But don't wait too long, the inventory turns over quickly at The Booksmith. Most topics are available with the main emphasis placed on fiction.

Established in 1979, The Booksmith is wheelchair accessible. They do have a small art gallery that is up three steps. The 19th and 20th century prints are completely in view of a person who can't navigate the three steps. Employees are happy to show you anything out of reach.

The Bookstore

General   475 Main St.
                                              Glen Ellyn, IL 60137
                                              708-469-2891
                                              <u>Hours:</u> Mon.- Wed., Fri. 9-5:30;
                                              Thurs. 9-9

"Dedicated to the Fine Art of Browsing," is how owners Dwight and Barbara Reed describe The Bookstore in suburban Glen Ellyn. To achieve this vision, they stocked over 12,000 titles and have developed an inviting store ambiance with plenty of seating to welcome "our guests", as the Reeds refer to their customers. Soft easy listening music plays throughout the store. The staff is happy to extend personalized attention when desired.

The Bookstore stocks books to please general interests and features an extra-special children's department. The "Bookstore Bear" welcomes children to their separate section of books. The store will special order books listed in "Books in Print". Magazines and greeting cards are also available in the store. Local authors are spotlighted by autographing sessions.

The store is "80%" wheelchair accessible inside and fully accessible from the outside. Discounts are extended on quantity orders and to libraries and schools.

Next time you are in the western suburbs and would like to further develop your fine art of browsing expertise, visit the Bookstore.

Borders Book Shop

General

1600 16th Street
Oak Brook, IL 60521
708-574-0800
Hours: Mon.-Sat 9-9; Sun. 11-6

Borders Book Shop is located in the Oaks of Oak Brook shopping center (on Route 83 just south of Routes 56 and 38) and is the dream shop of any book lover. Borders' two stories of towering shelves hold over 110,000 titles. If, by some strange chance, they don't have the book you need, special orders are no problem.

Whatever topic you're interested in, Borders Book Shop has a department filled with titles. Because each translation of foreign classics slightly differs depending upon the translator, Borders will often stock several translations of the same work. For example, Borders stocks five different translations of Tolstoy's "War and Peace." Whether you choose a copy by the translator, or by the critical notes attached, or even the design on the cover, Borders has a book to fit your wants. If you read foreign languages, you'll enjoy the entire shelf devoted to literature in other languages.

In addition to a number of unadvertised sale books, Borders Book Shop routinely offers a 30% discount on New York Times and Chicago Tribune hardback best sellers and 10% off most other hardbacks. One bookcase is devoted to selections recommended by the staff of Borders and they also carry a 30% discount tag. Also for sale are a great selection of both common and hard-to-find magazines and greeting cards.

To accommodate all the books, Borders has two full stories of bookcases neatly organized and attractively designed. You can rise to the second floor by escalator, stairs, or elevator. Among the many departments found upstairs is the incredible children's section. They have from 12-14,000 children's books and have a free story telling time every other Saturday. Famous characters often stop by to surprise the young shoppers. Curious George was a recent visitor.

Borders Book Shop makes the customer their number one concern. They were one of the first bookstores to include ample seating in the store. It's easy to spend hours browsing at Borders and the chairs and benches are appreciated by many. Wheelchair shoppers can glide through the store easily. Using a wheelchair myself, I've often been approached by a smiling employee who offered assistance in reaching books on upper shelves or moving a bench that might be in the way. Borders makes their customers comfortable. They even have two bathrooms with handicapped grab-bars available.

Many special services are extended to customers: mail and phone orders, gift wrapping, bestselling author autographing sessions, frequent live musicians, a newsletter, and authentic artwork for sale which features area artists.

Borders Book Shop was founded in Ann Arbor, Michigan and is continuing to expand. This is the only Borders site in the Chicago area. Having Borders in the western suburb of Oak Brook is like having a downtown gigantic bookstore nearby. As more book lovers discover Borders, the store continues to gain more and more browsers. Fortunately, check-out is relatively fast.

Whenever you have time to spare or feel like investigating the books that are on the market, Borders Book Shop is the place to go.

Centuries & Sleuths Bookstore

History & Mystery

743 Garfield
Oak Park, IL 60304
708-848-7243
Hours: Mon., Thurs., Fri. 11-9;
Tues. Wed. 11-7; Sat. 10-5;
Sun. noon-5

After some 500 years, the Centuries & Sleuths Bookstore jury has found Richard III not guilty of kidnapping, murder, and treason. On July 28, 1991, history came alive as The Trial of Richard III was performed ad-lib by real lawyers, a jury, and a real judge, the Honorable Eugene Wedoff. Witnesses testified and calmly discussed their lives and deaths. About 75 people attended the unrehearsed production and excitedly discussed prospective topics for another such event.

This was just one of many activities conducted by owner August Aleksy and his wife, Tracy, that makes Centuries & Sleuths a lively bookstore. Earlier in 1991, they presented a 5 foot by 9 foot diorama of the Battle of Waterloo which included over 2,000 miniature hand-painted figures, discussions such as "The History of Mystery," a children's story time, author autographing sessions, Sherlock Holmes presentations, and a historical discussion group. Plans are underway to develop a mystery discussion group. To help their patrons stay aware of their variety of activities, they publish a newsletter.

Physically, this classically traditional bookstore has a Bruce plaid carpet framed with forest green. The green walls are lined with rich wood bookcases filled with the reason you visit Centuries & Sleuths--books. Church pews, Windsor chairs and Board of Directors chairs are scattered throughout the store for the comfort of clients. You'll find patrons leisurely reviewing books or debating with another patron about some time in the near or distant past.

The book selection is excellent. With over 3,500 titles in stock, you're sure to find the history and mystery book you've been wanting. The heading "history" includes biographies, historical fine art, archaeology, historical economics, music, medicine, religion, women's studies, gay issues, cookbooks, militaria and philosophy. You'll find travel, tourism, cooking, and children's books relating to both history and mystery. Also in stock are University Press books, brass bookmarks, adult and children t-shirts with the distinctive Centuries & Sleuths logo.

On top of this, Centuries & Sleuths has a discount program called the Literature Club. If you make twelve purchases of ten dollars or more within six months, you receive five dollars off your next purchase of ten dollars or more. The store is located just south of the Eisenhower and is wheelchair accessible. Parking is available on the side streets nearby.

"We are a full service bookstore. but yes, we have deceived you if you believe we are only a place to order something, browse, and pay for a book," said August Aleksy III, proprietor. "We're out to get you - involved!"

It's no mystery that you're drawn to Centuries & Sleuths; they're a terrific bookstore and more.

Chicago Zoological Park Bookstore

Zoology

3300 Golf Rd.
Brookfield, IL 60513
708-485-0236, X 580
Hours: Summer: Daily 10-6;
Winter: Daily 10-5

Not only will you enjoy the historic Brookfield Zoo, you'll really enjoy their bookshop which is the largest zoo bookstore in the world.

Naturally, the focus of the store is animal, zoological, and nature related. Books specifically oriented toward children are available. Primates, birds, mammals and reptiles are the celebrities of the over 4,000 titles of books. Discounts are available to zoo, school, and public libraries. Special orders are taken on books in print.

Like the entire zoo, the bookstore is wheelchair accessible with bathrooms available for the disabled.

From aardvarks to zebras, you'll find out all about them here. Be sure to stop by whenever you're visiting friends in the zoo.

Churchmart

Religious   25W560 Geneva Rd. PO Box 66
                                              Wheaton, IL 60189
                                              708-653-6010
                                              Hours: Mon.-Fri. 8-4:30

A discount Christian bookstore, Churchmart, offers a 20% discount on most of their stock of Bibles and Christian literature. They stock 5,000 titles but have access to many more.

Mostly operating as a mail order service, Churchmart is wheelchair accessible. They sell Sunday school curriculums to churches and individuals. Also for sale are music compact discs, printed sheet music, and computer software designed especially for churches.

Cross Reference Bookstore

Religious   630 N. Lake St.
                                              Aurora, IL 60506
                                              708-892-8759
                                              Hours: Mon.-Thurs. 9:30-6;
                                              Fri. 9:30-7; Sat. 9-5

Cross Reference Bookstore stocks over 4,000 titles relating to Christian fiction, reference, children's books, self-help, cults, family studies, and Bible studies. In addition to books, they sell music on cassettes and compact discs, Precious Moments, assorted gifts, and a full line of choir robes.

Owners Charlotte and Dennis Hess defined the store motto as "Serving Him by serving His people." They strive for this ideal by making the store comfortable for all shoppers, offering senior citizens a discount and making free deliveries to hospitals and nursing homes in the community. The store is wheelchair accessible and everyone strives to make the store comfortable for all customers.

The store will celebrate it's eighteenth year in business in 1992. They also have two branches located in Oswego and Sandwich, Illinois.

Crown Books

General

156F East Lake St.
Bloomingdale, IL 60108
708-894-5663
<u>Hours:</u> Mon.-Fri. 10-9;
Sat. 10-6; Sun. 11-5

Crown Books

General

1324 Butterfield Rd.
Downers Grove, IL 60515
708-629-8988
<u>Hours:</u> Mon.-Fri. 10-9;
Sat. 10-6; Sun. 11-5

Crown Books

General

7305 Lemont Rd. B-24
Downers Grove, IL 60515
708-971-8737
<u>Hours:</u> Mon.-Fri. 10-9;
Sat. 10-6; Sun. 11-5

Crown Books

General

303 S. Route 83
Elmhurst, IL 60126
708-279-9889
<u>Hours:</u> Mon.-Fri. 10-9;
Sat. 10-6; Sun. 11-5

Crown Books

General

Grant Square
Hinsdale, IL 60521
708-323-5745
<u>Hours:</u> Mon.-Fri. 10-9;
Sat. 10-6; Sun. 11-5

Crown Books

General

523 E. Roosevelt Road
Lombard, IL 60148
708-916-8766
<u>Hours:</u> Mon.-Fri. 10-9;
Sat. 10-6; Sun. 11-5

Crown Books

General

2340 Harlem Ave.
N. Riverside, IL 60546
708-447-7939
<u>Hours:</u> Mon.-Fri. 10-9;
Sat. 10-6; Sun. 11-5

Crown Books

General

572 S. Rte. 59
Naperville, IL 60540
708-357-5505
<u>Hours:</u> Mon.-Fri. 10-9;
Sat. 10-6; Sun. 11-5

Crown Books

General

1205 E. Ogden Avenue
Naperville, IL 60540
708-357-8110
<u>Hours:</u> Mon.-Fri. 10-9;
Sat. 10-6; Sun. 11-5

Crown Books

General

7119 W. North Ave.
Oak Park, IL 60302
708-848-8822
<u>Hours:</u> Mon.-Fri. 10-9;
Sat. 10-6; Sun. 11-5

Crown Books

General

43-A Garden Market Ctr.
Western Springs, IL 60558
708-246-9161
Hours: Mon.-Fri. 10-9;
Sat. 10-6; Sun. 11-5

Crown Books

General

254 E. Geneva Rd.
Wheaton, IL 60188
708-653-8988
Hours: Mon.-Fri. 10-9;
Sat. 10-6; Sun. 11-5

Crown Books

General

82 Danada Sq. W.
Wheaton, IL 60187
708-668-4770
Hours: Mon.-Fri. 10-9;
Sat. 10-6; Sun. 11-5

DeVry Institute of Tech. Bookstore

Text, Electronics

2000 S. Finley Rd.
Lombard, IL 60148
708-953-1300
Hours: Weekdays 8:45-1,
1:30-4:15 (additional Tues. &
Wed. evening 5:30-7)

Although the bookstore caters to students of DeVry Institute of Technology, they are also open to the public. The other locations of the school and bookstore; the other is at 3300 North Campbell in Chicago.

Books stocked cover electronics, computers, accounting, and business. Other items carried are calculators, tape recorders, oscilloscopes, electronic templates, mechanical drafting paper and assorted supplies.
Located inside the institute, the bookstore is wheelchair accessible.

Estate Books

Americana

5827 Burr Oak
Berkeley, IL 60163
708-547-6239
Hours: Mail order only

Conducting business by phone and mail order, Estate Books specializes in Americana and in particular, the Civil War. They also have many juvenile books. They have been in business for sixteen years and offer free lists to those interested.
Estate Books is especially interested in selling and buying books about Jesse Stuart. Check your shelves.

Family Bookstore

Religious

1168 Fox Valley Ctr.
Aurora, IL 60504
708-898-8400
Hours: Mon.-Fri. 10-9; Sat. 10-6

Family Bookstore is a chain of Christian bookstores with nine locations in the Chicagoland area. Kirk Ford, manager of the Fox Valley Center branch described the mission of the stores as "increasing the distribution of scripture-based products."
Topics of Christian books include Bibles, religion, Christian living, family and parenting, devotionals, Bible study guides, psychology, reference, fiction, children's books, and audio books on tape. Some of the books are written in Spanish.
Other items for sale are Christian gifts, printed and taped music, children's toys and games, T-shirts, greeting cards, and church supplies. Services are many: Bible name imprinting, ordering Sunday School curriculum and Vacation Bible School material, and choir robes and church supplies.
A ten percent discount is given when orders of ten or more of the same item are ordered. They also have special discount stamps for church libraries.
Nationwide, the Family Bookstore chain has approximately 125 stores. The stores carry basically the same items and offer the same services. You may want to call ahead to confirm wheelchair accessibility.

Family Bookstore

Religious

1554 W. Butterfield Rd.
Finley Sq.
Downers Grove, IL 60515
708-620-8600
<u>Hours:</u> Mon.-Fri. 10-9; Sat. 10-6

Please refer to the description of Family Bookstore above.

Family Bookstore

Religious

16 Countryside Plaza
Countryside, IL 60521
708-354-5660
<u>Hours:</u> Mon.-Fri. 10-9; Sat. 10-6

Please refer to the description of Family Bookstore above.

Family Bookstore

Religious

151 Rice Lake Square
Wheaton, IL 60187
708-682-8868
<u>Hours:</u> Mon.-Sat. 10-9;

Please refer to the description of Family Bookstore above.

His Place Christian Bookstore

Religion

808 Arlington
La Grange, IL 60525
708-354-1695
<u>Hours:</u> Mon.-Wed., Fri.
9:30-5:30; Thurs. 9:30-8:30;
Sat. 9:30-5

Located in a charming old building with high ceilings, His Place
Christian Bookstore is a comfortable place to browse through the books

and gifts. With a religious theme, the store has gathered a collection of books addressing biography, fiction, women's studies, health-nutrition, music, theology, children's books, mystery, romance, and some books in large type print.

The gift section has solutions to all your gift giving worries. For the new baby you can choose a little lamb that plays "Jesus Loves Me" or a darling Precious Moments figurine. For a wedding gift you may buy plaques with the marriage prayer inscribed or an afghan or wedding clock. You'll find something for every occasion: anniversaries, birthdays, baptisms, and those special times you like to surprise a friend or loved one.

The store is wheelchair accessible. Discounts are given to churches and members of the Precious Moments club. Special orders are no problem and usually arrive within four days.

Joe's Books

General
819 S. Oak Park Ave.
Oak Park, IL 60304
708-383-3338
Hours: Mon.-Fri. 11:30-7;
Sat. 9:30-5:30

Joe's Books are ready to become your books. Specializing in cinema and film books, Joe says he has a large selection of first edition fiction titles.

Also for sale are original movie posters from the 1930's and 1940's. Other lithographs are also for sale in this bright and roomy store.

In stock are over 18,000 titles at inexpensive prices. The store also has a book search service. According to Joe, the store is not accessible to wheelchairs from the outside but it's aisles are clear on the inside of the store.

John William Martin, Bookseller

Antiquarian
231 S. LaGrange Rd.
La Grange, IL 60525
708-352-8115
Hours: Appointment only

"I specialize in British and American literature, rare books, and first editions from 1600 to the present," said John William Martin, Bookseller extraordinare.

In addition, John says that he "drifts into some areas by design (who can separate 17th century literature from religion), or by chance (I have a fondness for emblem books)."

Collectors and other antiquarians appreciate the beautiful hardbound and leatherbound first editions and special editions. Some of the books are limited runs and/or author autographed copies. In addition to carrying books by specific authors, John also carries books about books, literary biographies, and literary criticism. For the scholar, you'll find books printed in Greek, Latin, and modern European languages.

Holding a PhD. in English from the University of Oregon, John has intensely studied quality antiquarian books which enables him to do appraisals. His business was established in 1973 and he carries approximately 10,000 titles.

John runs his business on an appointment basis. He is interested in buying antiquarian books as well as selling them. He often attends and bids at the major British and American auction houses.

If you are a connoisseur of books, you'll be delighted to speak with John. His business is not wheelchair accessible but when you call John you may be able to make special arrangements.

John's Family Bookshop Inc.

Religious
55 North Avenue
Glendale Hts., IL 60139
708-653-4244
Hours: Mon.-Fri. 9:30-8;
Sat. 9:30-5:30

Joyce Klein Bookseller

Antiquarian
818 North Blvd.
Oak Park, IL 60301
708-383-3033
Hours: Tues.-Sat. 10-6;
Sun. 11-3

Joyce Klein's little treasures are over 2,500 out-of-print cookbooks and a large group of children's books. Her store is comfortable, and filled with beautiful antiques, antique jewelry and glassware. Joyce has from 8-10,000 additional books available but not in the store. Many sales are conducted by mail order.

The front of the store has one step but wheelchairs can enter through the back door.

Karl's Kollectables

Antiquarian

Riverside Antiques
Piano Factory
St. Charles, IL 60174
708-377-7730
Hours: Daily 10-5

This may come as a shock to Chicagoans, but there is more to Illinois than Chicago. Collecting information, maps, and over 50,000 postcards about small towns in Illinois is Karl's Kollectables' specialty.

Located in picturesque St. Charles, the store is in a shopping center converted from an old piano factory. With over 2,000 books, Karl's Kollectables also has ephemera from the World's Fair, train time-tables from the 1940-50's, and old newspapers.

Although the store is on the third floor of the Piano Factory, don't be discouraged. There are two elevators and the store is wheelchair accessible.

Kroch's & Brentano's Inc.

General

2284 Fox Valley Center
Aurora, IL 60505
708-851-7773
Hours: Mon.-Fri. 10-9;
Sat. 10-6; Sun. 11-5

Kroch's & Brentano's Inc.

General

500 Oak Brook Center
Oak Brook, IL 60521
708-574-0340
Hours: Mon.-Fri. 10-9;
Sat. 10-6; Sun. 11-5

Kroch's & Brentano's Inc.

General

1028 Lake Street
Oak Park, IL 60301
708-848-9003
Hours: Mon., Thurs., Fri. 10-9;
Tues., Wed., Sat. 10-5:30; Sun.
noon-5

Left Bank Bookstall

General

104 S. Oak Park Ave.
Oak Park, IL 60302
708-383-4700
Hours: Mon.-Fri. 12-8; Sat. 10-5;
Sun. by chance

"We pride ourselves on offering items that are unusual or out of the mainstream," said Carole Goodwin, co-owner of Left Bank Bookstall in suburban Oak Park.

They can also take pride in the way they treat their customers. The staff will notify patrons when particular books of interest come into stock. They sponsor author autographing sessions, play live music in the store, conduct poetry reading sessions, and publish a newsletter to keep patrons informed.

Topics of the 15,000 books on their shelves include history, mystery, religion, women's studies, gay issues, and foreign literature in English. They also carry a line of new magazines that Carole describes as "unusual titles in music, politics, environment, and literature."

Ten percent discounts are given to libraries, schools, and other institutions. The store is wheelchair accessible. They have been in business since 1978.

Lemstone Books

Religious

210 Stratford Square Mall
Bloomingdale, IL 60108
708-351-4333
Hours: Mon.-Fri. 10-9;
Sat. 10-6; Sun. 11-5

The Little Book Shop Inc.

General

13 W. First St.
Hinsdale, IL 60521
708-323-1059
Hours: Mon.-Wed., Fri. 9-5:30;
Thurs. 9-8; Sat. 9-5

Phyllis Forward and Caroline Wheeler have developed a wonderful little book store in the heart of Hinsdale. With over 21,000 titles, the store's strong departments are children's books, art, and travel. They also stock many large print books, most in popular fiction.

The store recently began publishing a newsletter to keep patrons informed of sales, children's story hours, new book arrivals, and selections in their own book-of-the-month specials. The store has always had strong patronage from the Hinsdale community. Their service is excellent and they will special order books.

The Little Book Shop has been a book lover's tradition for many years and, hopefully many years to come.

Little Professor Book Center

General

Market Meadows
1261 Naper Blvd.
Naperville, IL 60540
708-961-2772
Hours: Mon.-Fri. 10-9;
Sat. 10-6; Sun. 12-5

"We romance our customers," said David Bridges, manager of the Little Professor Book Center in suburban Naperville. Those services include two-to-three days delivery on many specially ordered books, free gift wrapping, out-of-print searching, research services for businesses, schools, and individuals, mailing anywhere, and conducting book fairs.

With over 10,000 titles in stock, they offer all best sellers at discounted prices and children's hard cover books at 20% discounts. They also have established a Baker's Dozen Book Club and sponsor author autographing sessions, along with children's story-telling and reading groups.

Two sections of the Little Professor Book Center add to the uniqueness of the store. One department carries large print books not always offered at other bookstores. The second is the marvelous selections under the heading of "Recovery" which includes books for recovering addicts of all kinds. The Little Professor Book Center also sells greeting cards, maps, book marks, and a copying service.

Located in an outdoor mall, the store is close to parking, including handicapped parking. The store has close aisles but is wheelchair accessible if you don't have the leg extending foot-rests.

Loaves and Fishes

Religious   7 East First St.
                                               Hinsdale, IL 60521
                                               708-325-8448
                                               Hours: Mon.-Sat. 9:30-5:30;
                                               Thurs. 9:30-8

Located in downtown Hinsdale, Loaves and Fishes is a Christian bookstore that also carries many gifts which include decorative tin containers, pictures, greeting cards, music cassettes, and compact discs. Bible imprinting is a service offered.

This cozy little shop has a few steps to enter, making it impossible for wheelchairs.

Logos of Oak Park

Religious   101 N. Oak Park Ave.
                                               Oak Park, IL 60301
                                               708-848-6644
                                               Hours: Tues., Wed., Fri. 10-6;
                                               Mon. & Thurs. 10-8; Sat. 9:30-5

"We are a general bookstore specializing in Christian books and music," reported Marietta Walsh, co-owner of Logos of Oak Park. "We also carry a large recovery section of self-help books for Alcoholics Anonymous, Adult Children of Alcoholics, Overeater's Anonymous, etc."

Naturally, Bibles are the main focus of the store. They carry a large selection of Bibles for all denominations and the staff is knowledgeable and helpful if you have any questions. Personalized imprinting on Bibles is available.

You can telephone Logos of Oak Park, order a book as a gift, and they will gift wrap it and even mail it for you. Special orders usually take one week. Logos of Oak Park sponsors author autographing sessions and children's story telling times.

Along with the religious and recovery books, are children's books, humorous books, local interest books (such as Frank Lloyd Wright books), in addition to greeting cards, stationery, and assorted gifts.

The store is wheelchair accessible. Off-street parking is available and mass transit is close.

Magic Tree Bookstore

Children's

141 N. Oak Park Ave.
Oak Park, IL 60301
708-848-0770
Hours: Mon., Thurs., Fri. 10-8;
Tues., Wed., Sat. 10-6;
Sun. noon-4

Magic Tree Bookstore not only sells books, they develop young writers. They offer four week creative writing workshops for children. They even sponsor a young writer's support group that offers a forum for writers who happen to be children. The three owners of Magic Tree Bookstore, Iris Yippi, Rose Joseph, and Jan Shoup, believe in children and have developed a bookstore that is dedicated to quality and diversity, not quantity. Many books are published by small presses and carry multicultural themes. The classics are of particular interest in the store. They also have a good selection of parenting books.

In business since 1984, Magic Tree Bookstore offers a free storytelling time three times per week. Additional merchandise includes book-related stuffed animals, puppets, puzzles, and both audio and video tapes.

The store is open everyday and is wheelchair accessible. Although the store is physically small, it's beautifully decorated and a wonderfully encouraging atmosphere for children.

Matthew's Loyola Univ. Health Science Bookstore

Medical Texts

2160 S. First Ave.
Bldg. 123, Corridor C
Maywood, IL 60153
708-531-2062
Hours: Mon.-Fri. 8-5:30

Matthew's Loyola University Health Science Bookstore carries over 3,000 titles of medical, dental, and nursing books and a variety of medical equipment. In addition to sales of equipment, repairs can be done here. Also available are collegiate clothing, office supplies, greeting cards, and candy to feed a late-night cramming student.

The store offers monthly special discounts on selected merchandise. There is one step to get into the store and it is wheelchair accessible from that point. They do special order books and will send them anywhere in the continental United States.

The store was established in 1985 and is a branch of a company that is 100 years old. There are sixteen other branches nationwide.

Matthews CCOM Bookstore

Texts

555 31st St.
Downers Grove, IL 60515
708-515-6143
Hours: Mon.-Fri. 10-6

"As a medical bookstore located inside a swiftly expanding osteopathic college," Manager Mark A. Hamilton said, "our focus is medical but we always get into discussions about current news, politics, children, and music."

"Our bookstore has become a meeting place of many minds and ideas and even of other cultures," he continued. Students are from all over the country.

Mark proudly said that the college is expanding and will soon add a Pharmacy school. The school hopes to attain university status.

The bookstore is dedicated to supplying their students with the right tools: medical, psychology, health-nutrition and reference books as well as medical clothing, instruments, medical posters and gifts, greeting cards, and school supplies. Of course, no school bookstore is complete without a shelf of candy, juice, nuts, and gum. As an extra service, the bookstore sells postage stamps. Clothes are always offered at a 20% discount.

Wheelchairs are no problem at this bookstore. Parking is off-street and mass transit is available. Stop by Matthews CCOM Bookstore and join the discussion.

Michele's Book Exchange & Gifts

Used

217 S. Villa Ave.
Villa Park, IL 60181
708-833-6009
Hours: Mon.-Fri. 10-6; Sat. 10-5;
call for Sun. hours

"We are people oriented," says Michele Mahoney, owner of Michele's Book Exchange and Gifts. "We enjoy 'the browser' as much as 'the buyer'."

Michele has a variety of used books and the volume is constantly changing. She estimates more than 15,000 books are in stock all the time. The selection includes the following topics: mystery, fiction, romance, fine art, biography, cookery, antiques, and children's books.

But the store has more: costume jewelry, handcrafted items, "Memories of Yesterday" and "Kinka" figurines, wall decorations, unusual greeting cards. Michele notes that her store is connected to The Oak

Tree Antique store and a stop at her shop makes for a day of fun for browsing.

The store is wheelchair accessible, but cautious Michele reports that off-street parking is across a busy street. If you are looking for gift items, take your chances with the busy street. You'll be happy you did.

Never Never Land

Children's

112 N. Hale Street
Wheaton, IL 60187
708-690-7909
Hours: Mon. & Thurs. 9:30-9;
Tues., Wed., Fri., Sat. 9:30-5:30

All children know of the famed Never, Never Land, where Peter Pan lives, as a place where you never have to grow up. A visit to Never, Never Land in Wheaton will delight your children and return friends that you thought had long disappeared. You can enjoy watching your children meeting such friends from your childhood as Curious George, Clifford, and Madeline. Over 8,500 titles are in stock.

"Our employees keep current on all new books and issues in children's bookselling so that we may better help our customers," says owner Patty Beachler Toht.

In the fall of 1991, Never, Never Land moved to their new location which is a combination toy store/book store. The two areas are separate and distinct but make for an easy one-stop shopping. Patty notes that children delight in the activities that combine reading with a particular activity such as cooking, magic, gardening, and even learning a foreign language. Girls in early grade school love the new series called "American Girls" which features characters their own age from the past so they can learn about growing up in different time periods in America.

Never, Never Land conducts free story-telling time each Wednesday morning. Occasionally they hold author autographing sessions. A newsletter keeps everyone informed as to the special activities and recent book releases. The store also has free gift wrapping.

In addition to books and toys, Never, Never Land sells music cassettes, some videos, audio books, and posters for children. Discounts are offered to teachers for school use. The store is wheelchair accessible.

"We can make knowledgeable recommendations for different ages to help find the special book for a child you love," Patty adds.

North Central College Bookstore

Text

30 N. Brainard St.
Naperville, IL 60566
708-420-0060
<u>Hours:</u> Mon.-Thurs. 9-5;
Fri. 10-2; Summer: Mon.-Thurs.
10-6; Fri. 10-2

The North Central College Bookstore is a must stop if you're a student at the college. Most of the stock is new and used textbooks. If you're not a student and like to collect college sweat-shirts, T-shirts, and gift items, you'll enjoy this bookstore.

With three to seven steps required to enter the store, it is not wheelchair accessible. It is a member of the Follett's College chain.

Novel Ideas

Used

63rd & Woodward
Downers Grove, IL 60515
708-963-8480
<u>Hours:</u> Tues.-Sat. 10-5

Recently expanded, Novel Ideas stocks from 75,000 to 100,000 used paperback books all in good quality. The popular topics are science fiction, mystery, romance, and fiction. Bring paperbacks that you would like to trade and you'll receive credit toward your purchases. Established in 1976, Novel Ideas is wheelchair accessible.

Owen Davies Bookseller

Transportation

200 W. Harrison St.
Oak Park, IL 60304
708-848-1186
<u>Hours:</u> Tues.-Sat. 9-4:30;
mail order

Owen Davies can take you on a sentimental journey when you visit his store. His books all focus on transportation, especially trains and ships. He even has time tables, menus, photographs, and magazines. A catalogue is published four times per year. The business is open Tuesday through Saturday and by phone and mail order. For those in a wheelchair, Owen says getting around the store is tricky.

Paperback Peddlers

Used

975 Aurora Ave.
Aurora, IL 60505
708-897-6622
Hours: Mon.-Fri. 10-8;
Sat. 10-5; Sun. noon-4

When you need to clean out your old paperbacks to find room for new books consider bringing them to Paperback Peddlers. They are ready to give you a credit toward your next purchase of twenty percent of the cover price of books. The store has hundreds of used paperbacks from which to choose. Also for sale are greeting cards and comic books. The store is wheelchair accessible.

Persistence of Memory

Used

3222 S. Harlem Ave.
Riverside, IL 60546
708-442-0667
Hours: Mon.-Fri. 11:30-7;
Sat. 11-7; Sun. 12-5

"We try to provide something for everyone from romance to occult to children's books," says John Montes, owner of Persistence of Memory bookstore. "We have a price range from forty cents for our Blue Star Specials to signed first editions and beautiful coffee table art books."

Over 12,500 used hardback and paperbacks are stocked inside Persistence of Memory's 700 square feet. Other departments they are proud of include history, mystery, literature, militaria, and science fiction. If you're a geography nut, they also have a huge selection of National Geographic magazines.

Persistence of Memory sponsors 20% off sales and coupons at various times. They do a book search for you for only 75 cents. For the comfort of browsers, they have some seating available.

Unfortunately, Persistence of Memory has three steps to enter the store and is therefore not wheelchair accessible. The store was established in 1989.

Quest Bookshop

Metaphysics

306 W. Geneva Rd.
Wheaton, IL 60187
708-665-0130
Hours: Mon., Tues., Wed., Fri.
10-6; Thurs. 10-8; Sat. 10-5;
Sun. 1:30-5; mail order

Quest sells books of poetry, ancient wisdoms, health and healing, environmental issues, prose, and associated arts.

The store, located on a forty acre tract of land in suburban Wheaton, also sells natural oils, jewelry, crystals, video and music cassettes. The store is wheelchair accessible, although there is a small curb to navigate.

There is also a by-mail lending library that you can join. Call 708-668-1571 for further information.

Restoration Book Shoppe

Religious

17W697 Ste. E. Roosevelt Rd.
Oakbrook Terr., IL 60181
708-629-2665
Hours: Mon., Thurs., Fri. 9-9;
Tues., Wed. 9-6; Sat. 9-6

If the family Bible that you inherited is beginning to show it's age, perhaps it needs some loving care. The Restoration Book Shoppe knows just how to fix your treasure. If your church is planning to have a special program, call Restoration Book Shoppe and they will set up a table with books for sale that highlights the topic of the program.

Restoration Book Shoppe sells over 500 titles of Christian books, Bibles and many other items. They include T-shirts, stationery, coffee mugs, bookmarks, wedding and baby gifts, music cassette tapes and compact discs, greeting cards, and posters. A video tape rental and sales program has been established. They will special order books in print.

The store is wheelchair accessible and is open six days per week.

Richard Owen Roberts Booksellers

Antiquarian

P. O. Box 21
Wheaton, IL 60181
708-584-8069
Hours: Appointment and mail
order only

"We are theological specialists with considerable holdings in other areas," said Richard O. Roberts, bookseller.

Principally a mail-order business, he also carries books on biography, history, social sciences, psychology, education, philosophy, reference, archeology, music, and some books in French and German.

An antiquarian and used book dealer since 1961, Richard O. Roberts is also able to appraise the value of books you have in your library.

Rizzoli Bookstore

General

294 Oak Brook Center
Oak Brook, IL 60521
708-574-6900
Hours: Mon.-Fri. 10-9;
Sat. 10-6; Sun. noon-5

A wonderfully comfortable store, Rizzoli Bookstore is one of the more popular spots in Oak Brook Center. The store has a huge selection of books for general interest and particularly special fine arts, architecture, and interior design sections. Gift books abound.

The store is located on two levels with an elevator and staircase to the second floor. Wheelchairs have no problems anywhere in Rizzoli Bookstore. The design of the store is attractive and airy.

In addition to their fantastic selection of books, they also have a large music section filled with compact discs and cassette tapes. Their selection is extensive in jazz, opera, classics, international, and Broadway hits. Also for sale are blank books with beautiful bindings, stationery, greeting cards, foreign newspapers and a few foreign magazines.

When you are in Oak Brook, it's worth your time to stop at Rizzoli Bookstore, especially if you're looking for a special gift for someone.

Robert Mueller Rare Books

Antiquarian   8124 W. 26th St.
                                 N. Riverside, IL 60546
                                 708-447-6441
                                 <u>Hours:</u> Appointment only

Robert Mueller describes his business as a "small, select stock of antiquarian books and first editions sold from my home."

He caters to collectors who have unconventional attitudes toward book collecting. He would rather track down a lesser known regional author than a Hemingway. Topics he's found recently include arts and crafts, history, mystery, social sciences, fine art, children's books, fiction, horticulture, literature, philosophy, reference, cinema, performing art, and local interest. He also sells books about books to those in the book trade.

In business for eleven years, he has built a fine reputation for selling books in excellent condition. He is always pleased to assist the collector in collection development. He offers an unconditional guarantee and will ship books upon request.

"I'm pleased to buy or sell a single volume or a collection," Robert said.

If you are new to book collecting or have an established library, you'll enjoy speaking with this interesting and friendly gentleman.

Robin's Bookshop Ltd.

General   220 S. Third St.
                                 Geneva, IL 60134
                                 708-232-0222
                                 <u>Hours:</u> Mon.-Sat. 9:30-5:30;
                                 Sun. 1-4

Geneva is a lovely little town that has numerous specialty shops located in historic houses. If you've never been to Geneva, you may wish to spend a full day visiting. If you are a book lover, you will want to first stop at Robin's Bookstore which is in an 1850 Greek revival style home that now holds 15-20,000 books between its walls.

The home feeling is maintained inside as you zig-zag through the various rooms. The front room has a beautiful antique fireplace that roars during cold days. Among the selections in the front room is a small but very high quality collection of business books. The coffee table highlights gift books and near the front door are discounted books and a travel section. You'll be able to find books in many categories including fiction, fine arts, architecture, inspirational, and a huge children's section in the back of the house. The children's section also carries beautiful figurines and dishes of Beatrix Potter and Winnie-the-Pooh characters.

Although Robin's Bookshop hasn't always been located in the historic home, the bookstore itself has been in business for 65 years. The bookshop is wheelchair accessible inside if you can manage one big back door step; the front has three steps to enter.

Robin's Bookshop recently acquired a toll free number for those wishing to place a phone order. The number is 1-800-433-3796. Mail order is also available.

This wonderfully attractive and friendly store is a delight to visit. You'll love sinking into the comfy chairs in the front room while you browse the excellent selection. Even non-book lovers enjoy this shop.

Salmagundi

Mystery
10324 Route 59, (at 103rd St.)
Naperville, IL 60564
708-904-4656
Hours: Mon., Tues., Wed., Fri.
10-6:30; Thurs. 10-8; Sat. 9-5;
Sun open in fall

A mystery lover's dream is Salmagundi. It's location? Route 59 and 103rd Street in the western suburb of Naperville. Take a nice drive through the countryside and you'll find something for everyone at Salmagundi.

The name of the store means "mixture" and Salmagundi has a delightful mixture of mystery books, unique children's books, gifts, picture frames and art prints. According to owners Lynn and Jim Crandall, you can find something special for everyone on your shopping list in all price ranges from 95 cents to $5,000.

Stepping into Salmagundi for the first time, you'll be charmed by the pleasant employees and talented owners. The mystery books are displayed in a home-library setting with custom made wooden bookcases lining three huge walls filled with almost every mystery book in print by virtually every mystery writer imaginable. If you wonder what books to choose, ask an expert, Jim, who is probably close-by. Then sink into the wingbacked upholstered chairs near the fireplace to make your decisions. Like a cozy English-manor library, the book area is ideal.

In the children's section all the books are on low bookcases or decoratively placed on the floor, which makes for easy browsing for the kids. The treasures they'll discover include a multitude of educational and fun books. Lynn has also chosen a group of books regarding some of the more difficult aspects of life presented in sensitive formats for a child's understanding. Topics of these beautifully illustrated books include death, handicaps, divorce, etc.

Between the two specialized book departments, you'll find over 3,500 separate titles among the 12,000 volumes in stock. Salmagundi will happily order any book in print. Parking is extremely close since the 3,500 square-foot store is in a mini-mall setting of quaint Victorian architecture. The store is completely wheelchair accessible. Disabled parking and a ramp are located just around the corner from Salmagundi.

Salmagundi is not just a mixture of the two book genres. It has tastefully selected and beautifully displayed gifts of all sorts, most which are made in the United States.

"About 75% of our entire stock is handmade work by American craftsmen," Lynn explained. The workmanship in every piece is exquisite and prices extremely reasonable.

You'll find carved and painted ducks, small glass buildings shaped as Chicago's skyline, colored paperweights, brass and copper statuettes, cloth 3-dimensional parrots, wind chimes, clocks, stuffed animals and puppets, wooden toys, desk sets, and so much more. Some pieces have been imported from Ireland, Scotland, and England. If you're a collector of the detailed cottages by David Winter, you'll find every piece available here. Correia is a special glass that no one else within a 70 mile radius carries.

In the art section of the store, you'll find handtinted lithographs, reproductions, and even Egyptian hieroglyphics on actual papyrus. Most of the artwork is limited editions. Custom framing is also available with a wide selection of mattes and frames to choose from.

Lynn acknowledges that they know most of their customers and she knows just what pieces to purchase to delight patrons. At Christmas time she sells and displays elegant, unique Christmas ornaments with prices ranging from $5 to $15.

Decorated with the golden touch of an interior designer, Salmagundi is a wonderful shop to visit if you're in the mood for mystery books or unique, quality gifts. Be sure to introduce yourself to the delightful Lynn and Jim Crandall. They'll make you feel at home in their home-away-from-home.

School of Metaphysics Bookstore

2228 S. Highland
Berwyn, IL 60402
708-788-0674
Hours: Varies with school year.

Scripture Press Bookstore

Religious   1825 College Ave.
                                               Wheaton, IL 60187
                                               708-668-6001
                                               Hours: Mon.-Wed. & Fri. 9-6;
                                               Thurs. 9-9; Sat. 9-5

Delightful customer service is not the only reason you should visit Scripture Press Bookstore. Their collection of new books include Bibles, religion, music, reference, fiction, women's studies, psychology, and children's books. There are over 20,000 titles on the shelves. Also in stock are a variety of gifts, award items, cards, and stationery.

With their customers in mind, Scripture Press Bookstore publishes a newsletter to let patrons know about the special events they conduct: live music, author autographing, music parties and children's story telling.

They have a huge annual sale and unadvertised specials. Seniors receive discounts and if you're buying for a group, you may qualify for a ten percent discount.

The store is wheelchair accessible and off-street parking is available. They have been in business since 1941.

Thomas & Thomas Booksellers

Antiquarian   1138 Erie St.
                                               Oak Park, IL 60302
                                               708-848-9620
                                               Hours: Appointment and mail
                                               order only

With more than three thousand rare and out-of-print books about fine cookery and wine, Thomas & Thomas Booksellers conducts business by phone and mail order as well as by appointment. A catalogue is available.

Thomas W. Burrows Bookseller

Antiquarian   P.O. Box 400
                                               Downers Grove, IL 60515
                                               708-960-1028
                                               Hours: Appointment only

A librarian who can't seem to get his fill of books, Tom enjoys bookselling through the mail when time permits. His main interests includes the humanities, history, literature, religious, scholarly, and the classics. He occasionally distributes catalogs and lists. He has been a bookseller since 1971.

Toad Hall

General

121 W. Front St.
Wheaton, IL 60187
708-653-2830
Hours: Mon.-Sat. 9:30-9;
Sun. noon-5

Whenever you have been searching for a book and haven't been able to locate it, visit Toad Hall in suburban Wheaton. You'll be sure to find it there. There are over 40,000 titles in stock.

When I visited Toad Hall, a frantic man ran into the store and queried the owner. Pleading, the said he needed a book for his wife for her birthday. After only a few questions from the owner and five minutes, the man left Toad Hall feeling that he had the perfect gift book for his wife, one that was written just for her.

The subjects in stock cover all wide range of interests. Of special note are the business and science sections. The children have their own special section in a separate room at the back of the store.

Toad Hall is in a beautiful old building in quaint downtown Wheaton. The ceilings are high allowing books to grow like vines up the walls. The walls and carpeting are a deep, rich green and the store has open, airy feeling making for comfortable browsing.

Although the store entrance has three stairs to enter. Wheelchairers have no fear. You can use the ramp entrance at the back of the store (call ahead to make sure the door is left open) to enjoy hours of browsing at Toad Hall.

Town House Books

General

105 N. Second Ave.
Saint Charles, IL 60174
708-584-8600
Hours: Mon.-Sat. 9-6:30;
Sun. 12:30-4:30

With more than 30,000 books, Town House Books carries general interest books along with specializing in American Indian studies, nature, women's studies, and children's books. The store is wheelchair accessible. When you visit this bookstore, be sure to browse through the other specialty shops in this little town on the Fox River.

Twice Read Books

Used

124 Calendar Court
La Grange, IL 60525
708-352-8115
Hours: Mon.-Fri. 1pm-7pm;
Sat. 10-5:30

John William Martin likes books and people. Therefore, he has established a business to help the people he finds most interesting: book readers. With book readers' interests in mind, John says that he has found a secret source for obtaining some books about six months before they're available to other stores.

John's interest in book collecting began while he was earning his doctorate in English in 1971. He began selling books by mail in 1973. In 1989 he moved ("the worst experience in my life") to the store location on Calendar Court in LaGrange.

Over 40,000 titles of used and rare hardbacks and paperbacks are discounted. He also has a selection of new books at a fifty percent discount. There is hardly a topic you won't find at Twice Read Books. John also buys books in large and small quantities. As a rare book dealer, he is well acquainted with the scholastic research necessary for correctly appraising the value of a book.

The store is wheelchair accessible. The hours that Twice Read Books is open is atypical because John is also an English teacher at Moraine Valley Community College.

Village Book Nook

General

38 S. LaGrange Rd.
La Grange, IL 60525
708-354-1174
Hours: Mon.-Fri. 9:30-5:30;
Sat. 10-4

At the Village Book Nook in La Grange, you can browse through their 10,000 general interest titles. They have a large children's section. Special orders are usually received within one week of the order. An assortment of gifts and greeting cards are also for sale.

The store is wheelchair accessible.

Waldenbooks

General

2426 Fox Valley Center
Aurora, IL 60505
708-898-5800
Hours: Mon.-Fri. 10-9;
Sat. 10-5:30; Sun. 11-5

Waldenbooks

General

c/o Coles Stratford Square
Bloomingdale, IL 60108
708-893-7573
Hours: Mon.-Fri. 10-9;
Sat. 10-6; Sun. 11-5

Waldenbooks

General

185 Countryside Plaza,
LaGrange Rd.
La Grange, IL 60525
708-352-0255
Hours: Mon.-Fri. 10-9;
Sat. 10-6; Sun. 12-5

Waldenbooks

General

261 Yorktown Sq.
Lombard, IL 60148
708-627-1274
Hours: Mon.-Fri. 10-9;
Sat. 10-5:30; Sun. 11-5

Waldenbooks

General

N. Riverside Park
7501 W. Cermak
N. Riverside, IL 60546
708-447-5888
Hours: Mon.-Fri. 10-9;
Sat. 10-5:30; Sun. 11-5

Wheaton College Bookstore

Text

420 E. Franklin St.
Wheaton, IL 60187
708-260-5119
Hours: Mon. 9-8;
Tues.-Fri. 9-4:30, Sat. 10-2;
Summer Mon.-Fri. 9-4:30

In early 1992, the Wheaton College Bookstore will expand to 9,000 square feet which will enable them to quadruple the trade section. Currently, their main stock is academic books.

In addition to textbooks, they carry many reference books, literature, theology, and Christian/public policy issues. Faculty authors from Wheaton College find a home for their books in this bookstore. They carry special collections written by C.S. Lewis, Tolkien, and Chesterton. (To see a museum and research center focusing on these three authors, refer to the story about the Wade Center.)

Naturally, you'll also find various Wheaton College products at this bookstore. Author autographing sessions occur at times. Discounts are extended to faculty and staff of Wheaton College. On special occasions, alumni receive a discount.

The store is wheelchair accessible with off-street parking available. The campus is a 15-20 minute walk from the Wheaton train station. You'll enjoy roaming Wheaton's campus and residential streets afterwards.

Williams-Sonoma

Cooking, Nutrition

100 Oak Brook Center
Oak Brook, IL 60521
708-571-2702
Hours: Mon.-Fri. 10-9;
Sat. 10-6; Sun. 12-5

The Williams-Sonoma name should make your taste buds tingle. They specialize in gourmet cooking and have the books and cookware to achieve any wizardry you can create in your kitchen.

Ye Olde Book Worm

General

Plaza De Campana
229 W. Grand--QE
Bensenville, IL 60106
708-616-1590
Hours: Mon.-Fri. 11-7; Sat. 11-5

Ye Olde Book Worm is opening their new location in Bensenville and, by now, all the real book worms have found it's new home.

The store stocks 25,000 different titles and has quick access to an additional 60,000 titles in it's warehouse. The warehouse is not open to the public. Special orders are welcome and a search service for out-of-print books is available. As a special bonus to customers, Ye Olde Book Worm sponsors special author autographing sessions.

Senior citizens are given a 10% discount on new books and a 20% discount on used books. Special sale discounts are available periodically.

Quite a variety of books are available at Ye Olde Book Worm. Among the topics available are: fiction, history, literature, biography, business, photography, science fiction, cinema and film, mystery, reference and romance.

Off-street parking is available and the store is completely wheelchair accessible. Be sure to check out this new location.

Ziegler's Book Exchange

Used

28 S. Villa
Villa Park, IL 60181
708-832-1020
Hours: Sat. 10-3;
Mon. Wed.-Fri. 10-5:30;
closed Tuesday and Sunday

The Newberry Library

Not Just For Scholars

One of the most magnificent places for book lovers in Chicago is the Newberry Library. This isn't like any library you've ever experienced before. Of course you can "read a book, research a paper, or examine a manuscript," as the Library's brochure states. But the books you read may include rare first editions, your research source material may include map surveying of early explorations of the Chicago area, and the manuscript you examine may be illuminated pieces enscribed by monks who met their maker several centuries ago.

As one of the leading humanities research libraries in the United States, the Newberry Library offers even more than this. For example, there is a Saturday morning series of informal free lectures that are open to the public. Topics have included "Issues in Feminist Renaissance Literature," "Ecological History of the Louisiana Territory," "The Trial Court as an Arena for Cultural Beliefs and Challenges," and "Poetry: Its Popularity and Future Growth." Frequent display exhibits often highlight antique maps and art displays by members of the Chicago Calligraphy Collective. On weekdays, the Newberry Library offers a mid-morning lecture series which focuses on one of the Newberry's fine treasures. Newberry scholars conduct the presentations. There is a small fee for attending the lectures. Periodically, the Newberry Library also presents dramatic and musical performances.

There are many different memberships levels at which you can join the Library. Annual membership fees start at $35. All memberships include invitations to special events (lectures, exhibits, dramatic and musical performances, etc.), a free subscription to their newsletter, and discounts on Newberry tickets, tuition to their classes and purchases at their bookshop.

The Newberry Library is located at 60 West Walton Street in Chicago. The telephone number is (312) 943-9090. It is wheelchair accessible (use the North entrance).

Each August the Newberry conducts a well-organized book fair that continues to grow in popularity. You'll find terrific used books at incredibly low prices. The topics are diverse because the books for sale are all donated by book lovers. The proceeds go to support the Library's programs in the humanities.

According to a Newberry Library brochure: "Discover the cultural life of the Newberry. It's not just for reading anymore."

The Wade Center

Where Hobbits Take a Breather

Scholars from all parts of the world convene in a small section of the library on the campus of Wheaton College. They are drawn here to study seven British authors. What? British authors in Wheaton?

Even scholars from prestigious Oxford make their odyssey to the Marion E. Wade Center to pour over the outstanding collection of books and writings by and about Christian writers C.S. Lewis, J.R.R. Tolkien, Owen Barfield, G.K. Chesterton, Charles Williams, Dorothy L. Sayers and George MacDonald.

The collection includes over 25,000 letters, 500 manuscripts, 10,000 books, thousands of articles and periodicals, hundreds of dissertations, and several hundred photographs. Items may not be removed from the center but researchers are encouraged to make brief or extended visits.

The small museum is open to visitors to browse through the glass enclosed, beautifully bound books, touch the desks of C.S. Lewis and J.R.R. Tolkien and gaze at the wall tapestry of Dorothy L. Sayer. The original illustration by Pauline Baynes of the full-color map of C.S. Lewis's Narnia is displayed.

In 1965 Dr. Clyde S. Kilby, a Wheaton College professor of English and friend of C.S. Lewis, began collecting and preserving Lewis memorabilia. Kilby spent the summer of 1967 working with J.R.R. Tolkien on "The Silmarillion", making it ready for publication. Kilby's collection grew and grew. Wheaton College became interested and still supports the collection today.

In 1974, the family and friends of Mr. Marion E. Wade established the Wade Center in memory of his commitment to the promulgation of the books and ideas of C.S. Lewis and like-minded Christian authors. A yearly grant is provided in Marion E. Wade's memory. Additional funding for the center comes from the donations of individual supporters.

Today, the Marion E. Wade Center is open to the public at no charge. Group tours can be arranged with short notice. Programs and lectures are available to churches, private and public schools, seminaries, colleges, universities, clubs, and organizations. Lectures and seminars are given all across the globe.

A monthly discussion group of the Mythopoeic Society meets to discuss the authors highlighted at the Wade Center and related literary works. The group is open to new friends.

The Wade Center has a small gallery of postcards, gifts, books, and audio tapes of the annual Wade Lectures are available. You can also pick up free pamphlets describing the Wade Center and a list of recommended books for children.

When you visit Wade Center, you may be fortunate enough to meet Stephanie Feeck, a Collection Assistant. Stephanie delightfully tells visitors about the Wade Center and describes the museum pieces to interested visitors. Stephanie's love for C.S. Lewis' works began as a child when her favorite books were the "The Chronicles of Narnia." One piece she proudly discusses is a huge, hand-carved wardrobe made by C.S. Lewis' grandfather that had stood in the Lewis family home in Belfast, Ireland. As a child, C.S. Lewis would play in the wardrobe.

Today, the Wade Center has a sign on the wardrobe that states: "The Wade Center assumes no responsibility for persons who disappear or are lost." It's easy for any book lover to become lost in the wealth of resources available at the Wade Center.

The Wade Center is located on the Wheaton College campus and the telephone number is (708) 260-5908. The Center is wheelchair accessible.

Book Collecting

For the Really Serious Book Lover

If you are like me and treat your books like true treasures, you may be on the brink of book collecting. As a hobby, book collecting is something you can do anywhere in the country and you can be a collector without investing a huge amount of money.

Your book collection is a personal reflection of you because you choose what to collect. Some collectors choose a particular subject or author to collect. Some collect any first editions, or author autographed copies, or even paperbacks.

First Editions

For a collector, first edition means the first time a book was printed. It's the edition that was printed closest to the time that the book was actually written. The author may even have guided it's production.

When determining the value of a book, antiquarians review many factors including the quality of the book and the popularity of the author. A first edition copy of John J. Audubon's *Birds of North America* was valued at $500 in 1939. Today the book is valued at approximately $25,000.

Take a second look at Mom's copy of Margaret Mitchell's Gone With the Wind, copyright May, 1936. Today it's worth $2,000.

Authors you're sure to recognize whose hard-cover first edition books are currently selling for $30-$50 include Isaac Asimov, Joseph Heller, Flannery O'Connor, Philip Roth, John Updike and Kurt Vonnegut.

Reference books you can use to determine the value of first editions are: *First Editions: A Guide to Identification* by Edward N. Zempel and Linda A. Verkely (published by The Spoon River Press, Box 3635, Peoria, IL, 61614) and *A Pocket Guide to the Identification of First Editions* by Bill McBride (available from the author at 157 Sisson Ave., Hartford, CT 06105.) The reference collections of libraries often include price guides to first editions.

Proofs and Advance Review Copies

Before a book is released to the mass market, copies are distributed to book reviewers, bookstore owners, and managers. These copies are often unedited galley proofs and can look very different from the final product. Very few of these editions are published and their value varies. A large science fiction collection of these is located at Chicago Historical Bookworks in Evanston.

Limited Editions

Limited Edition books are usually signed and numbered in a slipcase, and cost three to five times the cost of the mass market first edition. Often these books are printed on fine paper and have ornate covers.

Many organizations exist that work solely with top quality limited editions. One company, named Limited Editions Club (LEC) was established in 1929. You may also want to check books published by Heritage Press, Franklin Press, Trade Book Publishers, and Fine Press Books.

Sources

If you're serious about getting involved in book collecting, you'll first want to obtain a copy of the Antiquarian Booksellers Association of America (ABAA) listing of it's members. Their address is ABAA, 50 Rockefeller Plaza, New York, NY 10020. Armed with this directory, you have an excuse to travel all across the country consulting with antiquarians. For your convenience, you will find many antiquarians of Chicagoland listed in this book.

Often antiquarians operate their businesses from their homes and meet by appointment only. Others publish catalogues and operate mail order businesses. Some antiquarians specialize in specific book fields by becoming experts in that one area. They may not stock books in other fields. With a little research, you can find the specialist in your field of interest. *The Book Lover's Guide* can help you do this.

Other sources to which you can turn are the many used book stores, library sales, antique stores, and even garage sales. Prices in different parts of the country vary due to local market demands.

Want to check out the incredibly expensive books? Drop in to auctions held at Swann Galleries, Christie's and Sotheby's, all of which are located in New York.

If you are interested in pursuing book collecting, many books are available for your study. Below is an abbreviated bibliography of helpful books:

Ahearn, Allen. *Book Collecting: A Comprehensive Guide.* New York: G.P. Putnam's Sons, 1989.

Carter, John. *ABC for Book Collectors.* London: Hart-Davis, MacGibbon, 1974.

Dunbar, Maurice. *Fundamentals of Book Collecting.* Los Altos, CA: Hermes Publications, 1976.

McBride, Bill. *A Pocket Guide to the Identification of First Editions.* Hartford, CT: McBride/Publisher, 1985.

Minters, Arthur H. *Collecting Books for Fun and Profit.* New York: Arco Publishers, 1979.

Zempel, Edward N., and Linda A. Verkler. *A First Edition?* Peoria, IL: Spoon River Press, 1985.

Printers Row Book Fair

Come to the Fair!

In mid-June there is one outdoor event that brings book lovers of all varieties into the sunlight. It's the Printers Row Book Fair. Bookstore owners bring their wares and book lovers bring their checkbooks. When the two forces hit head-on, you know what happens: fun for everyone.

First held in 1985, the Printers Row Book Fair has developed into the United States' third largest book fair. It is a two-day event that includes more than 150 book sellers and publishers selling their wares on Dearborn Street from the Congress Parkway to Polk Street. But there is more than just books here. Authors read selections from their work (Kurt Vonnegut was 1991's star). Poets have an open microphone in a tent where they can read their own work. Panels discuss the hottest issues facing authors, publishers, and readers. Special programs for children are also conducted. The fair stages demonstrations of bookbinding, calligraphy, marbling, and papermaking. No admission is charged.

The Book Fair is held in Chicago's historic printing district, Printers Row. If you have never ventured to this part of Chicago, you must. Many bookstores and stationery shops have found homes. The Printers Row Printing Museum at 731 South Plymouth Court is a fascinating place that reviews the history of printing. During the Book Fair, Johannes Guttenberg himself made an appearance and printed a page from his bible.

The fair is sponsored by the Mayor's Office of Special Events, the Department of Cultural Affairs, the Chicago Board of Trade, and the Illinois Arts Council. For information contact the Burnham Park Planning Board at (312) 987-1980.

Custom Bookcases

A Home for Your Books

So now that you have visited all the bookstores in Chicagoland and have risked bankruptcy by buying so many books, what in the world are you going to do with those books sitting on the living room floor, the kitchen table, and even the bathroom sink?

Of course bookcases are the solution. But three or four shelves just won't hold all of your books. Do what the bookstores do. Consider the benefits of custom-made bookcases. You can have cases built to that reach your ceilings, shorter shelves for paperbacks, display easels for special books, even include a television and VCR shelf. When you are the designer, all things are possible. You can even have a traditional rolling ladder included in your personal library. When you choose a professional bookcase-maker, you know you'll receive quality craftsmanship.

I'm aware of two companies that specialize in custom bookcases and entertainment centers. They have made bookcases for libraries, professional offices, bookstores, and private homes.

First is The Bookcase Company, located at 701 North State Street in Elgin, Illinois 60120. Representatives will travel to many parts of Chicagoland. Call them at (708) 888-5858. Most business is conducted by appointment.

Another company is New England Woodworking Ltd. Their address is 24 Center Drive, Unit #1, Gilberts, Illinois 60136. Gilberts is a small town in Kane County. The phone number is (708) 428-7634. They also have a shop-at-home service and conduct appointments in the evening if it's more convenient for you.

If you have always dreamed of living in a library, your wishes may come true with just a phone call.

Continuing Your Education

A Life of the Mind

Your education shouldn't end on graduation day. For many, graduation marks the day you can grow from one phase of your life to another. The University of Chicago offers an adult education program which ignores textbooks and pop quizzes and focuses on informative, sometimes heated, discussions of the classics of the western tradition.

Known as "The Basic Program," the four-year program involves and challenges each person to develop themselves through discussion of universal problems of humankind. The lively discussions and challenging encounters with fascinating people are brought together to cultivate intellectual growth.

The brochure describes the program best: "The first-year texts explore the operations of guilt and innocence, freedom and conscience, justice, and the law within society, while the second-year readings address the related problem of knowledge and responsibility. Texts to be read in the third-year sections focus on power and leadership, and the fourth-year readings concentrate on the human impulse leading us to leave a record of our observations for those who come after."

The curriculum has developed to include the works of Aristotle, Plato, Socrates, Homer, Shakespeare, Chaucer, Kant, Hume, Nietzsche, Pascal, Machiavelli, Darwin, Freud, Dostoevsky, Dante, Swift, Austen, Marx, and even Mark Twain. The topics include philosophy, religion, politics, history, psychology, drama, and fiction.

The Basic Program is conducted at three locations: the Fine Arts Building on South Michigan Avenue, the University of Chicago campus in Hyde Park, and at the University of Chicago Graduate School of Business on the Near North side. The groups come together once per week either on a weekday (you can choose either evening or midday classes) or on a Saturday morning.

Alumni courses are open to those who have completed two or more years of the prescribed four-year curriculum. The Alumni Courses allow students to study an author in greater depth and complement the Basic Program. Some topics in the past have included the Great Essayists, Myths, Tragedies, and Epics, Lincoln and the Slavery Question, Plato's Dialogues, the Arabian Nights, Ancient Historians, James Joyce's Ulysses, and Henry James.

Class sizes is restricted to twenty-five students to allow participation from everyone. Contact the Basic Program offices (312-702-1727) for fee and schedule information.

If you don't have enough time to join the Basic Program, the University of Chicago offers free lectures open to the public on the first Friday of every month. The lectures last for one hour and are held at the Chicago Public Library Cultural Center.

Also free of charge and open to the public are a series of lectures titled "The Works of the Mind Lectures." Held on the University of Chicago campus, the lectures last 1-2 hours, are followed with a discussion and include light refreshments. All the lectures are conducted by professors at the University of Chicago or Basic Program staff members.

Although Ray Ciacci, a Basic Program Chairman for five years, was discussing the Basic Program, the following 1990 quote is reflective of all the Adult Education Programs held by the University of Chicago: "The pleasure lies in the examination, the exploration, and the challenge that these seminal thinkers pose. For a mature, intelligent person to grapple with the best minds of the Western intellectual tradition is a joy."

Calligraphy

Lovelier Than Just Words

"Calligraphy is the art of writing beautifully," Marc Drogin, master calligrapher, wrote in his book *Medieval Calligraphy*.

"It is the written letter, molded by one's concept of ultimate grace and perfect balance, a personal artistic expression as unique as the lines on the fingertips with which one holds the pen. It places one's soul at the tip of the pen for all to see," Drogin added.

Calligraphy has come to us thanks to the scribes of the Middle Ages. The beautifully written words are our only record of the faraway past. Many of the classic works of Greece and Rome survived the ravages of time and the destruction of the Library at Alexandria due to their dedication and artistry. Still, comparatively few uncut manuscripts have survived to the present. Although their work is not for sale, you can see some beautiful pieces on display at The Graphic Conservation Department of R.R. Donnelley & Sons, Inc. at 223 Martin Luther King Drive in Chicago. The Newberry Library has a magnificent collection (the largest outside England) and they exhibit works by modern calligraphers and members of the Chicago Calligraphy Collective. A few rare book collectors also have pages of authentic hand-written pieces for sale. George Ritzlin in Highland Park, for example, has a nice collection.

Chicago is fortunate to be the home of one of the few businesses in the United States which is dedicated to creating modern calligraphic pieces that challenge the monks in quality and style. B.C. Kassell Company, founded in 1901, is a small group of artists that create heirlooms and awards at reasonable prices.

Johnny A. Perez and his wife, Anna de Perez, are the owners of B.C. Kassell Company today. Both artists create works that draw praise from anyone who sees their work. Johnny's work has been exhibited five times at the Smithsonian Institute in Washington, D.C. He has created a music award given to Elvis Presley, a memorial book for President Johnson's library, and an invitation from the City of Chicago to Queen Elizabeth II. His work hangs in countries all over the world from the English Parliament to corridors in Israel, Mexico, and Hong Kong.

In the studio, six experienced scribes using the techniques and styles of monks mix their own colors and add real gold to illuminate the projects. Pieces are completely hand-drawn, lettered, and illuminated on fine parchment papers.

Clients can visit the studio to discuss projects, review samples, and choose the designs they prefer for their individual pieces. Whether the occasion calls for simple and inexpensive work or the most elaborate, B.C. Kassel Company artists will create the piece to suit your needs. One artist works on each piece from beginning to magnificent completion.

Johnny creates much of his work in his studio at home. All the pieces require extreme concentration and extraordinary skill. Johnny explains that one decorative letter on a page can take an hour to a full week to create depending upon the intricacy of the design.

Today, B.C. Kassel Company performs their magic on diplomas, certificates, and awards. Pieces can be created for any purpose and say anything that suits your needs.

"I work to satisfy my own taste and then I know the customer will be happy," said Johnny. If you are an artist, you know that this is a tall order. Many of the greatest artists were never pleased with their own creations.

B.C. Kassell is located at 29 E. Madison Street, Suite 900, in Chicago IL 60602. Their phone number is 312-236-3965. If you commission them to create a piece of art for you, you'll be thrilled with a work that may just last for centuries.

Chicagoland Libraries

As book lovers, we hold as an article of faith that libraries are a joy and a blessing. All those books to read for free (or at worst a nominal fee).

In an age of shrinking municipal resources, Chicago is fortunate to have a major new addition to our library family. In October 1991 the new Harold Washington Library Center opened in the South Loop. This new library is 10 stories tall and contains 750,000 square feet. Most important of all, the new $144 million library will house 2 million books, which makes it the largest library in the Midwest.

The birth of this building was a prolonged affair. In the early 1980's it looked like the library would be housed in the old Goldblatt Building. Once the decision was made to build a new library, the design of the new building became an *event*. The PBS program Nova even dedicated an episode to the competition among architects for the contract.

Still, all is not unalloyed joy in the universe of Chicagoland's libraries. Many are facing very difficult choices, given their budget constraints. Too many libraries believe that their resources are treasures that should be jealously guarded and hoarded. For example, fewer and fewer libraries allow unhindered access to and browsing of magazine back issues. Now the libraries compel you to determine in advance which magazines you wish to browse, stand in line for five minutes, fill out a form, wait for the clerk to retrieve your magazines (no more than three at a time please!), go to a desk, discover that those magazines didn't interest you, stand in line again, and repeat the process. Hardly worth the effort. But at least those magazines are safe! Extraordinarily difficult to access, but safe! Some libraries vigorously defend this policy, despite the extra staff it requires. Next thing you know, they will be restricting access to their books, using the same rationale. Library users of the world, unite! You are in danger of losing your browsing rights!

Now, it may be impractical from a space point of view to give unrestricted access to several years of magazine back issues, but having no unrestricted access to back issues is absurd. The Wheaton Public Library, for example, will typically display several months worth of back issues of each magazine, making the library a much more valuable and friendly place. Let's hope that moore libraries follow their lead.

The Talking Book Center

Options for the Blind

If you can't climb the mountain, there are still many ways to get around to the other side. People with physical disabilities are constantly challenged to find creative ways to achieve the same goals as the able-bodied.

Established by Congress in 1931, The National Library Service for the Blind and Physically Handicapped has been developing resources to entertain and assist those who are physically challenged.

With the cooperation of authors and publishers, the National Library service selects and produces full-length books and magazines in braille and on recorded disc and cassette. The Chicago Public Library Talking Book Center delivers reading materials and playback machines to borrowers who have been recognized by the Library of Congress as a qualifying individual. The playback equipment is loaned free to readers for as long as they participate in the program. Equipment includes talking-book machines, cassette machines, breath switches, extension levers, pillow phones, remote-control units for those with limited mobility, and headphone amplifiers for those with hearing impairments.

Books are selected for the program on the basis of their appeal to a wide range of interests. Those in great demand include bestsellers, fiction, biographies, and how-to books. A limited number of books are produced in foreign languages. The program also contains approximately seventy popular magazines.

Each month participants receive a newsletter describing recent publications. They contact the Talking Book Center to receive selections of their choice. Postage-free mail and personal delivery ensure that cost is not an obstacle to the borrower. Currently, the national book collection contains over 59,000 titles and 13 million copies. Playback machines are kept by the library member and replaced and maintained by the library.

Musical scores are often impossible to read even for those with good eyesight. Now musical scores are available in braille and large type, as well as instruction manuals for voice, piano, guitar, and more.

Volunteers help to make the program a success. It is volunteers who record the tapes and proofread the braille. Free correspondence courses are available which lead to certification in braille transcription of literature and music. Volunteers also repair talking book and cassette machines.

Your public librarian can give you more details about the program and how to apply. If you prefer, you can contact the following offices for information.

Reference Section
National Library Service
for the Blind and Physically Handicapped
Library of Congress
Washington, D.C. 20542
(202) 707-5100.

Chicago Public Library
Talking Book Center
1055 W. Roosevelt Road
Chicago, IL 60608
(312) 738-9200

Other resources include:

Horizons for the Blind, Inc.
7001 N. Clark Street
Chicago, IL 60626
(312) 973-7600

Educational Tape Recording for the Blind
3915 West 103rd St.
Chicago, IL 60655
(312) 445-3533

Johanna Bureau for the Blind and Physically Handicapped, Inc.
8 S. Michigan Ave.
Chicago, IL 60603
(312) 332-6076

Artists Book Works

How to Build A Book

Many book lovers want to learn more about the manufacture of books. Artists Book Works conducts classes and workshops year round on different aspects of bookmaking as an art form. They are a center for promoting the art and craft of the handmade book.

Classes are held in papermaking, book arts, book repair, Japanese woodblock printing, marbling, making Mexican bark paper, bookbinding, and many other subjects. Classes are reasonably priced and include all the materials appropriate to the course. Class size is limited so each student is given personal attention. Before registering for a class, wheelchair users should speak with school representatives about accessibility. Some of the classrooms are very tight and others have room to accommodate wheelchairs.

Facilities at Artists Book Works include a letterpress studio with Vandercook Universal I and Pearl Platten presses, and a bookbinding studio with book presses, nipping presses, board shears, lying presses, and more. Members are allowed full access to the facilities to produce their own work.

Annually Artists Book Works sponsors the production of a limited edition book printed at their facility. A board of guest jurors select the lucky person who receives an honorarium for travel, materials, and technical assistance. If you are interested, send for information regarding the residency's guidelines and deadline. Be sure to enclose a self-addressed stamped envelope.

You can become a member of Artist Book Works on different categories. Membership costs from $30 to $1000. Members receive all mailings and discounts on classes and workshops. As your membership contribution increases, so do your benefits.

If you love books but don't want to do the actual work yourself, Artists Book Works does have a slide registry highlighting artists who craft books. Artists Book Works also conducts exhibits, lectures, art expos, and fairs.

The director of Artists Book Works is Barbara Metz and the Program Coordinator is Sabrena Nelson. The organization is non-profit and supported in part by the Illinois Arts Council. They can be reached at 1422 W. Irving Park Rd., Chicago, IL 60613. The phone number is 312-348-4469

Artists Book Works offers something of interest for everyone who cares about old books and the history of bookmaking. Whether you are looking for a new hobby or just admire and love books, you'll enjoy getting in touch with Artists Book Works.

Index of Stores by Specialty

Note: Some of the larger bookstores listed under the General category have a signficant selection of books covering virtually every category. Of special note are Borders and the flagship stores in the B. Dalton (Wabash address) and Kroch's & Brentano's (Wabash address) chains. For used books consider Booksellers Row (on Lincoln), Aspidistra, and O'Gara & Wilson.

Accounting

American Management Assoc Bookstore	*Chicago Northwest*
DeVry Bookstore	*Chicago Northwest*
DeVry Institute of Tech. Bookstore	*Western Suburbs*
National Louis University Bookstore	*Northern Suburbs*

Americana (also see Civil War)

Abraham Lincoln Book Shop	*Chicago Central*
American Opinion Book & Research	*Northern Suburbs*
Bits & Pieces of History	*Southern Suburbs*
Chicago Historical Bookworks	*Northern Suburbs*
Chicago Historical Museum	*Chicago North*
Estate Books	*Western Suburbs*
Historical Newspapers & Journals	*Northern Suburbs*
Hooked on History	*Northwest Suburbs*
Kenneth Nebenzahl Inc.	*Northern Suburbs*
Larry Law's Bookstore	*Chicago North*
Thomas Joyce and Company	*Chicago West*

Antiquarian

Alkahest Bookshop	*Northern Suburbs*
Abraham's Books	*Northern Suburbs*
Beasley Books	*Chicago North*
Booklegger's	*Chicago North*
Booksellers Row	*Chicago North*
The Bookworks	*Chicago North*

Hamill & Barker	*Northern Suburbs*
Harry L. Stern Ltd.	*Chicago Central*
Herbert Furse - Bookman	*Northern Suburbs*
John William Martin, Bookseller	*Western Suburbs*
Joyce Klein Bookseller	*Western Suburbs*
Karl's Kollectables	*Western Suburbs*
Kenneth Nebenzahl Inc.	*Northern Suburbs*
Leekley Books	*Northern Suburbs*
Louis Kiernan, Bookseller	*Chicago South*
The Memorabilia Corner	*Northern Suburbs*
N. Fagin Books	*Chicago Northwest*
Norma K. Adler Books	*Northern Suburbs*
O'Gara & Wilson Booksellers, Ltd.	*Chicago South*
Plain Tales Books	*Northwest Suburbs*
Persistence of Memory	*Western Suburbs*
Renaissance Books	*Northern Suburbs*
Richard Adamiak	*Chicago South*
Richard Cady Rare Books	*Chicago North*
Richard Owen Roberts Booksellers	*Western Suburbs*
Richard S. Barnes	*Northern Suburbs*
Robert Mueller Rare Books	*Western Suburbs*
Thomas & Thomas Booksellers	*Western Suburbs*
Thomas Joyce and Company	*Chicago West*
Thomas W. Burrows Bookseller	*Western Suburbs*
Titles Inc.	*Northern Suburb*

Antique

Articles of War Ltd.	*Northern Suburbs*
Beasley Books	*Chicago North*
Bookman's Alley	*Northern Suburbs*
Fiery Clock Face	*Chicago Central*
Harry L. Stern Ltd.	*Chicago Central*
The Memorabilia Corner	*Northern Suburbs*
Richard Adamiak	*Chicago South*
Richard S. Barnes	*Northern Suburbs*
Terra Museum of American Art Books	*Chicago Central*

Archaeology

American Indian Books	*Chicago Northwest*
Chicago Zoological Park Bookstore	*Western Suburbs*
N. Fagin Books	*Chicago Northwest*
The Suq-Oriental Institute	*Chicago South*

Architecture

Archicenter Bookstore	*Chicago Central*
The Bookworks	*Northern Suburbs*
The Bookworks	*Chicago North*
The Contract Design Center Bookshop	*Chicago Central*
Dan Behnke, Bookseller	*Chicago North*
Field Museum of History--Shop	*Chicago Central*
Hamill & Barker	*Northern Suburbs*
IL Institute of Technology Bookshop	*Chicago South*
Louis Kiernan, Bookseller	*Chicago South*
Prairie Avenue Bookshop	*Chicago Central*
Robin's Bookshop Ltd.	*Western Suburbs*
Terra Museum of American Art Books	*Chicago Central*

Art (Fine)

Art Institute of Chicago	*Chicago Central*
Artists Book Works	*Chicago North*
Booklegger's	*Chicago North*
Booknook Parnassus	*Northern Suburbs*
The Bookworks	*Chicago North*
Heartland Books	*Northwest Suburbs*
Helix Ltd.	*Chicago West*
Louis Kiernan, Bookseller	*Chicago South*
Michele's Book Exchange & Gifts	*Western Suburbs*
Museum of Contemp. Art Store	*Chicago Central*
N. Fagin Books	*Chicago Northwest*
Rizzoli Bookstore	*Chicago North, Western Suburbs*
Robin's Bookshop Ltd.	*Western Suburbs*
Sidney Johnson Bookseller	*Northwest Suburbs*
Stuart Brent	*Chicago North*
Terra Museum of American Art Books	*Chicago Central*
The Little Book Shop Inc.	*Western Suburbs*
W. Graham Arader III	*Chicago Central*
Women & Children First, Inc.	*Chicago North*

Art (Performing)

Act I Bookstore	*Chicago North*
Bits & Pieces of History	*Southern Suburbs*
Book Box--Shake, Rattle, & Read	*Chicago North*

The Bookworks	*Chicago North*
The Bookworks	*Northern Suburbs*
Larry Law's Bookstore	*Chicago North*
Metro Golden Memories	*Chicago Northwest*
Paul Rohe & Sons	*Chicago North*
Scenes Coffeehouse & Drama Bkstr.	*Chicago North*
Yesterday	*Chicago North*

Arts and Crafts

Artists Book Works	*Chicago North*
Books Off Berwyn	*Chicago North*
Borders Book Shop	*Western Suburbs*
Field Museum of History--Shop	*Chicago Central*
Frog Tool	*Chicago West*
Heartland Books	*Northwest Suburbs*
J. Togori	*Chicago North*
Lose's Book Nook	*Northwest Suburbs*
Prairie Avenue Bookshop	*Chicago Central*
Terra Museum of American Art Books	*Chicago Central*
The Contract Design Center Bookshop	*Chicago Central*

Audio Books

Bible Book Center	*Southern Suburbs*
Carpenter's Shop	*Northern Suburbs*
Christian Literature Center	*Southern Suburbs*
Encyclopaedia Britannica Retail Store	*Northwest Suburbs*
Lake Forest Bookstore	*Northern Suburbs*
Never Never Land	*Western Suburbs*

Automotive

A & A Prosser Booksellers	*Chicago Northwest*
Hamill & Barker	*Northern Suburbs*

Biography

Abraham Lincoln Book Shop	*Chicago Central*
American Opinion Book & Research	*Northern Suburbs*
The Book Inn	*Southern Suburbs*
Carpenter's Shop	*Northern Suburbs*

Anderson's Bookshop	*Western Suburbs*
Beck's Book Store (near Truman College)	*Chicago North*
Book Fair, Inc.	*Northern Suburbs*
The Book Vine for Children	*Northwest Suburbs*
Borders Book Shop	*Western Suburbs*
Calvary Bookstore	*Southern Suburbs*
Chicago Bibles & Books	*Chicago Northwest*
Chicago Zoological Park Bookstore	*Western Suburbs*
The Children's Bookstore	*Chicago North*
Cokesbury	*Northwest Suburbs*
Coopersmith's	*Northwest Suburbs*
Dan Behnke, Bookseller	*Chicago North*
Encyclopaedia Britannica Retail Store	*Northwest Suburbs*
Europa Bookstore	*Northern Suburbs*
Family Health Education Service	*Chicago South*
Field Museum of History--Shop	*Chicago Central*
Fiery Clock Face	*Chicago North*
Giant Book Warehouse	*Northern Suburbs*
Heartland Books	*Northwest Suburbs*
His Place Christian Bookstore	*Western Suburbs*
Joyce Klein Bookseller	*Western Suburbs*
Katzy Book Shop	*Southern Suburbs*
The Little Book Shop Inc.	*Western Suburbs*
Little Professor Book Center	*Western Suburbs*
Logos of Oak Park	*Western Suburbs*
Lose's Book Nook	*Northwest Suburbs*
Magic Tree Bookstore	*Western Suburbs*
Michele's Book Exchange & Gifts	*Western Suburbs*
Modern Bookstore	*Chicago South*
Never Never Land	*Western Suburbs*
Pied Piper Children's Bookstore	*Northern Suburbs*
Platypus Bookshop	*Northern Suburbs*
Robin's Bookshop Ltd.	*Western Suburbs*
Sandmeyer's Bookstore in Printer's Row	*Chicago Central*
Sidney Johnson Bookseller	*Northwest Suburbs*
Town House Books	*Western Suburbs*
Toad Hall	*Western Suburbs*
V & H Stationery Co. Book Dept.	*Chicago Southwest*
Village Book Nook	*Western Suburbs*
WaldenKids	*Northern Suburbs*
Waldenkids	*Northwest Suburbs*
Wee the People of the World	*Northern Suburbs*
Women & Children First, Inc.	*Chicago North*
World Journal & Bookstore	*Chicago South*
Yesterday	*Chicago North*

Cinema

Act I Books	*Chicago North*
Chinatown Book and Gifts	*Chicago South*
Guild Books	*Chicago North*
Helix Ltd.	*Chicago West*
Joe's Books	*Western Suburbs*
Metro Golden Memories	*Chicago Northwest*
Scenes Coffeehouse & Drama Bkstr.	*Chicago North*
Yesterday	*Chicago North*

Civil War

Abraham Lincoln Book Shop	*Chicago Central*
Articles of War Ltd.	*Northern Suburbs*
Bits & Pieces of History	*Southern Suburbs*
Chicago Historical Society Museum	*Chicago North*
Estate Books	*Western Suburbs*
Hooked on History	*Northwest Suburbs*

Computers

B. Dalton (Wabash address)	*Chicago Central*
Books & Bytes	*Western Suburbs*
Borders Book Shop	*Western Suburbs*
Encyclopaedia Britannica Retail Store	*Northwest Suburbs*
Kroch's & Brentano's (Wabash address)	*Chicago Central*
University of Chicago Book Store	*Chicago South*

Cookery

Book Box -- Shake, Rattle & Read	*Chicago North*
The Book Inn	*Southern Suburbs*
Chinatown Book and Gifts	*Chicago South*
Fiery Clock Face	*Chicago North*
Heartland Books	*Northwest Suburbs*
Joyce Klein Bookseller	*Western Suburbs*
Katzy Book Shop	*Southern Suburbs*
Kay's Treasured Kookbook Kollection	*Northern Suburbs*

Lose's Book Nook	*Northwest Suburbs*
Michele's Book Exchange & Gifts	*Western Suburbs*
Scholars' Books, Inc.	*Chicago South*
Season To Taste Books Ltd.	*Chicago North*
Thomas & Thomas Booksellers	*Western Suburbs*
Williams-Sonoma	*Chicago Central*
Williams-Sonoma	*Northwest Suburbs*
Williams-Sonoma	*Western Suburbs*

Electronics

Kroch's & Brentano's (Wabash address)	*Chicago Central*
DeVry Bookstore	*Chicago Northwest*
DeVry Institute of Tech. Bookstore	*Western Suburbs*
Helix Ltd.	*Chicago West*

Encyclopedia

African American Book Center	*Chicago South*
Encyclopaedia Britannica Retail Store	*Northwest Suburbs*
Family Health Education Service	*Chicago South*

Environment

Chicago Zoological Park Bookstore	*Western Suburbs*
Field Museum of History--Shop	*Chicago Central*
John T. Shedd Aquarium Sea Shop	*Chicago Central*
N. Fagin Books	*Chicago Northwest*
Platypus Bookshop	*Northern Suburbs*
Quest Bookshop	*Western Suburbs*

Fantasy

Alkahest Bookshop	*Northern Suburbs*
Beyond Tomorrow Science Fiction	*Northwest Suburbs*
Robert & Phyllis Weinberg Books	*Southern Suburbs*
The Stars Our Destination	*Chicago North*

Fashions/Textiles

The Contract Design Center Bookshop	*Chicago Central*
Rizzoli Bookstore	*Chicago North*
Rizzoli Bookstore	*Western Suburbs*

Foreign Language

Arcade Bookshop	*Chicago Northwest*
Articles of War Ltd.	*Northern Suburbs*
Beck's Book Store (Truman College)	*Chicago North*
Bible Book Center	*Southern Suburbs*
Chicago Hebrew Bookstore	*Chicago Northwest*
Chicago Bibles & Books	*Chicago Northwest*
Chinatown Book and Gifts	*Chicago South*
Christian Literature Center	*Southern Suburbs*
Draugus Lithuanian Daily Friend	*Chicago Southern*
Encyclopaedia Britannica Retail Store	*Northwest Suburbs*
Europa Bookstore	*Northern Suburbs*
Family Health Education Service	*Chicago South*
Guild Books	*Chicago North*
Hamakor Gallery, Ltd	*Northern Suburbs*
Hamill & Barker	*Northern Suburbs*
Impact Book Store	*Chicago Northwest*
J. Toguri Mercantile Co.	*Chicago North*
John William Martin, Bookseller	*Western Suburbs*
Kazi Publications Inc.	*Chicago Northwest*
Kroch's & Brentano's (Wabash address)	*Chicago Central*
Libreria Yuquiyu	*Chicago Northwest*
Marxist-Leninist Books	*Chicago West*
N. Fagin Books	*Chicago Northwest*
Never Never Land	*Western Suburbs*
Peking Book House	*Northern Suburbs*
Polonia Book Store ← POLISH	*Chicago Northwest*
Rosenblum's World of Judaica	*Chicago Northwest*
Scholars' Books, Inc.	*Chicago South*
The Children's Bookstore	*Chicago North*
The Suq-Oriental Institute	*Chicago South*
Trinity Beacon Bookstore	*Northern Suburbs*
Wheaton College Bookstore	*Western Suburbs*
World Journal & Bookstore	*Chicago South*

Games/Puzzles

A Child's Garden of Books	*Northwest Suburbs*
Field Museum of History--Shop	*Chicago Central*
Waukegan Bridge Center	*Northern Suburbs*
Yesterday	*Chicago North*

Gay and Lesbian

Barbara's Bookstore	*Chicago North & Central*
Barbara's Bookstore	*Western Suburbs*
Left Bank Bookstall	*Western Suburbs*
People Like Us Books	*Chicago North*
Unabridged Books Inc.	*Chicago North*

General

57th Street Books	*Chicago South*
Abraham's Books	*Northern Suburbs*
Alkahest Bookshop	*Northern Suburbs*
Anderson's Bookshop	*Western Suburbs*
Andrews & Rose Booksellers	*Southern Suburbs*
Annie's Book Stop Inc.	*Northern Suburbs*
Aspidistra Bookshop	*Chicago North*
B. Dalton Bookseller	*All*
Barbara's Bookstore	*Chicago Central*
Barbara's Bookstore	*Chicago North*
Barbara's Bookstore	*Western Suburbs*
Beck's Book Store (Loyola/Mallinckrodt)	*Northern Suburbs*
Beck's Book Store (Loyola University)	*Chicago North*
Beck's Book Store (NIU)	*Chicago North*
Beck's Book Store (H. Washington Col.)	*Chicago Central*
The Book Bin	*Northern Suburbs*
Book Box -- Shake, Rattle & Read	*Chicago North*
Book Stall at Chestnut Court, The	*Northern Suburbs*
Bookman's Alley	*Northern Suburbs*
Bookman's Corner	*Chicago North*
Books Off Berwyn	*Chicago North*
Books on Belmont	*Chicago North*
Booksellers Row	*Chicago North*
The Booksmith	*Western Suburbs*
The Bookstore	*Western Suburbs*
The Bookworks	*Chicago North*

Index of Book Stores by Specialty

Robin's Bookshop Ltd.	*Western Suburbs*
Saint Xavier College Bookstore	*Chicago Southwest*
Selected Works Bookstore	*Chicago North*
Seminary Cooperative Bookstore Inc	*Chicago South*
Sidney Johnson Bookseller	*Northwest Suburbs*
Spanish Speaking Book Store	*Chicago North*
Stuart Brent Books	*Chicago Central*
Titles Inc.	*Northern Suburbs*
Toad Hall	*Western Suburbs*
Town House Books	*Western Suburbs*
Twice Read Books	*Western Suburbs*
US Government Bookstore	*Chicago Central*
Univ. of Chicago Bookstore	*Chicago South*
UIC--Epi Center Bookstore	*Chicago West*
V & H Stationery Co. Book Dept.	*Chicago Southwest*
Village Book Nook	*Western Suburbs*
Waldenbooks	*All*
The White Elephant Shop	*Chicago North*
Women & Children First, Inc.	*Chicago North*
Ye Olde Book Worm	*Northwest Suburbs*

Geography

Encyclopaedia Britannica Retail Store	*Northwest Suburbs*
Rand McNally Map Store	*Chicago Central*

History

57th Street Books	*Chicago South*
Abraham Lincoln Book Shop	*Chicago Central*
African American Book Center	*Chicago South*
American Opinion Book & Research	*Northern Suburbs*
American Indian Books	*Chicago Northwest*
Articles of War Ltd.	*Northern Suburbs*
Bits & Pieces of History	*Southern Suburbs*
The Book Inn	*Southern Suburbs*
Centuries & Sleuths Bookstore	*Western Suburbs*
Coopersmith's	*Northwest Suburbs*
Dan Behnke, Bookseller	*Chicago North*
The Emperor's Headquarters	*Chicago Northwest*
Encyclopaedia Britannica Retail Store	*Northwest Suburbs*
Field Museum of History--Shop	*Chicago Central*
Guild Books	*Chicago North*
Harry L. Stern Ltd.	*Chicago Central*

Horror

Horticulture

Humanities

Richard S. Barnes	*Northern Suburbs*
Selected Works Bookstore	*Chicago North*
Seminary Cooperative Bookstore, Inc.	*Chicago South*
Thomas W. Burrows Bookseller	*Western Suburbs*
University of Chicago Book Store	*Chicago South*

Humor

Richard S. Barnes	*Northern Suburbs*

Illuminated Manuscripts

George Ritzlin Maps and Books	*Northern Suburbs*
Harry L. Stern Ltd.	*Chicago Central*

Labor/Marxism

Guild Books	*Chicago North*
Marxist-Lenist Books	*Chicago West*
Modern Bookstore	*Chicago South*
Revolution Books	*Chicago North*

Large Type Print

Chicago Bibles & Books	*Chicago Northwest*
Christian Literature Center	*Southern Suburbs*
Family Health Education Service	*Chicago South*
Lake Forest Bookstore, Inc.	*Western Suburbs*
Little Book Shop Inc., The	*Western Suburbs*
Little Professor Book Center	*Western Suburbs*

Law

Chicago Law Book Company	*Chicago Southwest*
IIT Chicago Kent Law College Books	*Chicago Central*
Richard Adamiak	*Chicago South*
Thomas Joyce and Company	*Chicago West*

Literature

57th Street Books	*Chicago South*
African American Book Center	*Chicago South*
Anne W. Leonard Books	*Chicago South*
Barbara's Bookstore	*Chicago North and Central*
Barbara's Bookstore	*Western Suburbs*
Beasley Books	*Chicago North*
Beck's Book Store (near Truman College)	*Chicago North*
Book Inn, The	*Southern Suburbs*
Booklegger's	*Chicago North*
Books Off Berwyn	*Chicago North*
Chandler's Book Dept.	*Northern Suburbs*
DePaul University Bookstore	*Chicago North*
Encyclopaedia Britannica Retail Store	*Northwest Suburbs*
Europa Bookstore	*Northern Suburbs*
Great Expectations	*Northern Suburbs*
Guild Books	*Chicago North*
Hamill & Barker	*Northern Suburbs*
Heartland Books	*Northwest Suburbs*
John William Martin, Bookseller	*Western Suburbs*
Louis Kiernan, Bookseller	*Chicago South*
Modern Bookstore	*Chicago South*
Norma K. Adler Books	*Northern Suburbs*
Peking Book House	*Northern Suburbs*
Persistence of Memory	*Western Suburbs*
Plain Tales Books	*Northwest Suburbs*
Preservation Bookshop	*Northern Suburbs*
Sandmeyer's Bookstore in Printer's Row	*Chicago Central*
Scenes Coffeehouse & Drama Bkstr.	*Chicago North*
Selected Works Bookstore	*Chicago North*
Seminary Cooperative Bookstore, Inc.	*Chicago South*
Thomas Joyce and Company	*Chicago West*
Thomas W. Burrows Bookseller	*Western Suburbs*
University of Chicago Book Store	*Chicago South*
Wheaton College Bookstore	*Western Suburbs*
Women & Children First, Inc.	*Chicago North*

Magazines

American Opinion Book & Research	*Northern Suburbs*
Aurum Solis Occult	*Chicago North*
Book Box -- Shake, Rattle & Read	*Chicago North*
Book Adventures	*Chicago North*

The Book Market	*Chicago Northwest*
Bookworks, The	*Northern Suburbs*
Borders Book Store	*Western Suburbs*
Chinatown Book and Gifts	*Chicago South*
Everybody's Bookstore	*Chicago Northwest*
Family Health Education Service	*Chicago South*
Guild Books	*Chicago North*
Left Bank Bookstall	*Western Suburbs*
Owen Davies Bookseller	*Western Suburbs*
Rainbow Island Books	*Chicago Northwest*
Rave	*Chicago North*
Scenes Coffeehouse & Drama Bkstr.	*Chicago North*
UIC--Epi Center Bookstore	*Chicago West*
University of Chicago Bookstore	*Chicago South*
Yesterday	*Chicago North*

Magic/Occult

Aurum Solis Occult	*Chicago North*
Bell, Book, & Candle	*Chicago North*
Book Market, The	*Chicago Northwest*
Bookworks, The	*Chicago North*
Magic Inc.	*Chicago Northwest*
The Occult Bookstore	*Chicago North*

Maps/Cartography

George Ritzlin Maps and Books	*Northern Suburbs*
Harry L. Stern Ltd.	*Chicago Central*
J.T. Monckton Ltd.	*Northern Suburbs*
Karl's Kollectables	*Western Suburbs*
Kenneth Nebenzahl Inc.	*Northern Suburbs*
Rand McNally Map Store	*Chicago Central*

Masonic

Ezra A. Cook	*Chicago Northwest*
Powner's	*Chicago Northwest*

Medical

Beck's Book Store (near Truman College)	*Chicago North*
Dr. Wm. M. Scholl Colg. of Pod. Med	*Chicago Central*
Logins Medical Ctr. Bookstore	*Chicago West*
Matthew's Loyola U. Health Science	*Western Suburbs*
Matthews Chicago CCOM Bookstore	*Western Suburbs*
Peking Book House	*Northern Suburbs*
Saint Xavier College Bookstore	*Chicago Southern*
Thomas Joyce and Company	*Chicago West*
UIC Health Science Bookstore	*Chicago West*
University of Chicago Bookstore	*Chicago South*
Victor Kahn, Medical Book Consultant	*Northwest Suburbs*

Metaphysics

Aurum Solis Occult	*Chicago North*
Bell, Book, & Candle	*Chicago North*
Bookworks, The	*Northern Suburbs*
Bookworks, The	*Chicago North*
Pathfinder Bookstore	*Chicago North*
Pyramid Book Mart Inc.	*Southern Suburbs*
Quest Bookshop	*Western Suburbs*
School of Metaphysics Bookstore	*Chicago North*
School of Metaphysics Bookstore	*Northwest Suburbs*
Science of Mind Bookshop	*Chicago Central*

Militaria

Abraham Lincoln Book Shop	*Chicago Central*
Anthony Maita	*Northern Suburbs*
Articles of War Ltd.	*Northern Suburbs*
Dan Behnke, Bookseller	*Chicago North*
Emperor's Headquarters, The	*Chicago Northwest*
Heartland Books	*Northwest Suburbs*
Hooked on History	*Northwest Suburbs*
Persistence of Memory	*Western Suburbs*

Music

African American Book Center	*Chicago South*

Aurum Solis Occult	*Chicago North*
Beasley Books	*Chicago North*
Book Box -- Shake, Rattle & Read	*Chicago North*
Bookman's Alley	*Northern Suburbs*
Carl Fischer Music Inc.	*Chicago Central*
Churchmart	*Western Suburbs*
Great Expectations	*Northern Suburbs*
Guild Books	*Chicago North*
His Place Christian Bookstore	*Western Suburbs*
Larry Law's Bookstore	*Chicago North*
Loaves and Fishes	*Western Suburbs*
Louis Kiernan, Bookseller	*Chicago South*
Never Never Land	*Western Suburbs*
Rave	*Chicago North*
Selected Works Bookstore	*Chicago North*

Mystery

Anne W. Leonard Books	*Chicago South*
Barbara's Bookstore	*Chicago North and Central*
Barbara's Bookstore	*Western Suburbs*
Centuries & Sleuths Bookstore	*Western Suburbs*
Heartland Books	*Northwest Suburbs*
I Love A Mystery Bookstore	*Chicago Central*
Katzy Book Shop	*Southern Suburbs*
Kenneth Nebenzahl Inc.	*Northern Suburbs*
Left Bank Bookstall	*Western Suburbs*
Lose's Book Nook	*Northwest Suburbs*
Michele's Book Exchange & Gifts	*Western Suburbs*
Mystery Loves Company	*Chicago North*
Nevermore Books	*Chicago North*
Novel Ideas	*Western Suburbs*
Paperback Paperback	*Northwest Suburbs*
Persistence of Memory	*Western Suburbs*
Preservation Bookshop	*Northern Suburbs*
Reader's Haven Paperback Book Excg.	*Northwest Suburbs*
Salmagundi	*Western Suburbs*
Sandpiper Books Inc.	*Northwest Suburbs*
Scotland Yard Books Ltd.	*Northern Suburbs*
Second Editions	*Northern Suburbs*

Magic Inc.	*Chicago Northwest*
Magic Tree Bookstore	*Western Suburbs*
O'Gara & Wilson Booksellers, Ltd.	*Chicago South*
Owen Davies Bookseller	*Western Suburbs*
Pathfinder Bookstore	*Chicago North*
Peking Book House	*Northern Suburbs*
Pyramid Book Mart Inc.	*Southern Suburbs*
Richard Cady Rare Books	*Chicago North*
Scholars' Books, Inc.	*Chicago South*
Thomas & Thomas Booksellers	*Western Suburbs*
Town House Books	*Western Suburbs*
Victor Kahn, Medical Book Consultant	*Northwest Suburbs*
Waukegan Bridge Center	*Northern Suburbs*

Philosophy

57th Street Bookstore	*Chicago South*
Aurum Solis Occult	*Chicago North*
Booklegger's	*Chicago North*
Chandler's Book Dept.	*Northern Suburbs*
Great Expectations	*Northern Suburbs*
John William Martin, Bookseller	*Western Suburbs*
Kazi Publications Inc.	*Chicago Northwest*
Louis Kiernan, Bookseller	*Chicago South*
Selected Works Bookstore	*Chicago North*
Seminary Cooperative Bookstore	*Chicago South*
Stern's Book Service	*Chicago North*

Photography

Bits & Pieces of History	*Southern Suburbs*
The Bookworks	*Northern Suburbs*
The Bookworks	*Chicago North*
Chicago Zoological Park Bookstore	*Western Suburbs*
Helix Ltd.	*Chicago West*

Psychology

Beck's Book Store (Truman College)	*Chicago North*
C.G. Jung Institute Bookstore	*Northern Suburbs*
Carpenter's Shop	*Northern Suburbs*

Religion

A & A Prosser Booksellers	*Chicago Northwest*
Alverno Religious Art & Books	*Chicago Northwest*
American Opinion Book & Research	*Northern Suburbs*
Arcade Bookshop	*Chicago Northwest*
Aurum Solis Occult	*Chicago North*
Bell, Book, & Candle	*Chicago North*
Best of Books	*Northern Suburbs*
Bible Book Center	*Southern Suburbs*
C.G. Jung Institute Bookstore	*Northern Suburbs*
Calvary Bookstore	*Southern Suburbs*
Carpenter's Shop	*Northern Suburbs*
Chicago Bibles & Books	*Chicago Northwest*
Chicago Hebrew Bookstore	*Chicago Northwest*
Christian Literature Center	*Southern Suburbs*
The Christian Shop, Ltd.	*Northwest Suburbs*
Churchmart	*Western Suburbs*
Cokesbury	*Northwest Suburbs*
Community Bible & Book Co., Inc.	*Chicago West*
Covenant Bookstore	*Chicago Northwest*
Cross Reference Bookstore	*Western Suburbs*
Earthen Vessels Ltd.	*Northwest Suburbs*
Family Bookstore	*Northwest Suburbs*
Family Bookstore	*Southern Suburbs*
Family Bookstore	*Western Suburbs*
Hamakor Gallery, Ltd.	*Northern Suburbs*
His Place Christian Bookstore	*Western Suburbs*
Impact Book Store	*Chicago Northwest*
J.F. Morrow & Sons	*Chicago Northwest*
Kazi Publications Inc.	*Chicago Northwest*
Left Bank Bookstall	*Western Suburbs*
Lemstone Books	*All*
Loaves and Fishes	*Western Suburbs*
Logos Unlimited Bookstore	*Northwest Suburbs*
Logos of Evanston	*Northern Suburbs*
Logos of Oak Park	*Western Suburbs*
Louis Kiernan, Bookseller	*Chicago South*
Marytown Gift Shop	*Northern Suburbs*
Missions Possible Bookstore	*Northern Suburbs*
Moody Bookstore	*Chicago Central*
The Mustard Seed Christian Bookstore	*Chicago North*
National Chr. Bks-Gifts Dist. Inc.	*Chicago Northwest*
New Words of Wisdom Books Ltd. Inc.	*Northern Suburbs*
The Occult Bookstore	*Chicago North*
The Olive Branch, Ltd.	*Northwest Suburbs*
Restoration Book Shoppe	*Western Suburbs*

Romance

Science

Science Fiction

Beyond Tomorrow Science Fiction	*Northwest Suburbs*
Chicago Historical Bookworks	*Northern Suburbs*
Lose's Book Nook	*Northwest Suburbs*
Michele's Book Exchange & Gifts	*Western Suburbs*
Novel Ideas	*Western Suburbs*
Paperback Paperback	*Northwest Suburbs*
Persistence of Memory	*Western Suburbs*
Preservation Bookshop	*Northern Suburbs*
Robert & Phyllis Weinberg Books	*Southern Suburbs*
Sandpiper Books Inc.	*Northwest Suburbs*
The Stars Our Destination	*Chicago North*
Yesterday	*Chicago North*

Social Sciences

Beck's Book Store (Truman College)	*Chicago North*
The Carpenter's Shop	*Northern Suburbs*
Chandler's Book Dept.	*Northern Suburbs*
Guild Books	*Chicago North*
Modern Bookstore	*Chicago South*
N. Fagin Books	*Chicago Northwest*
National Louis University Bookstore	*Northern Suburbs*
Scholars' Books, Inc.	*Chicago South*
Seminary Cooperative Bookstore	*Chicago South*
Women & Children First, Inc.	*Chicago North*

Sports

Anne W. Leonard Books	*Chicago South*
The Bookworks	*Northern Suburbs*
The Bookworks	*Chicago North*
Dan Behnke, Bookseller	*Chicago North*
Lose's Book Nook	*Northwest Suburbs*
Yesterday	*Chicago North*

Technical

Borders Book Shop	*Western Suburbs*
IIT Bookshop	*Chicago South*
Kroch's & Brentano's (on Wabash)	*Chicago Central*
University of Chicago Bookstore	*Chicago South*

Textbooks

Barat College Bookstore	*Northern Suburbs*
Beck's Book Store (H. Washington Col.)	*Chicago Central*
Beck's Book Store (NIU)	*Chicago North*
Beck's Book Store (Loyola University)	*Chicago North*
Beck's Book Store (Loyola/Mallinckrodt)	*Northern Suburbs*
Beck's Book Store (Truman College)	*Chicago North*
Chandler's Bookstore	*Northern Suburbs*
Columbia College Bookstore	*Chicago Central*
Covenant Bookstore	*Chicago Northwest*
DePaul University Bookstore	*Chicago North*
DeVry Institute of Tech. Bookstore	*Western Suburbs*
DeVry Bookstore	*Chicago Northwest*
IIT Chicago Kent Law College Books	*Chicago Central*
IIT Bookshop	*Chicago South*
Kennedy-King College (C&W Books)	*Chicago Southwest*
Lake Forest College Bookstore	*Northern Suburbs*
Libreria Yuquiyu	*Chicago Northwest*
Logins Medical Center Bookstore	*Chicago West*
Malcom X College (C&W Books Ltd.)	*Chicago West*
Matthew's Loyola U. Health Science	*Western Suburbs*
Matthews Chicago CentralOM Bookstore	*Western Suburbs*
National Louis University Bookstore	*Northern Suburbs*
North Central College Bookstore	*Western Suburbs*
Olive-Harvey College (C&W Books)	*Chicago South*
Psychology Book Store Inc.	*Chicago Central*
R.J. Daley College (C&W Books Ltd.)	*Chicago Southwest*
Robert Morris College Bookstore	*Chicago Central*
Roosevelt University Bookstore	*Chicago Central*
Saint Xavier College Bookstore	*Chicago Southwest*
UIC--Epi Center Bookstore	*Chicago West*
Wheaton College Bookstore	*Western Suburbs*

Theatre/Plays - see also Art (Performance)

Act I Books	*Chicago North*
Scenes Coffeehouse & Drama Bkstr.	*Chicago North*
Yesterday	*Chicago North*

Transportation

Owen Davies   *Western Suburbs*

Travel and Tourism

Barbara's Bookstore	*Chicago North and Central*
Barbara's Bookstore	*Western Suburbs*
The Bookstore at Chestnut Court	*Northern Suburbs*
Chicago Zoological Park Bookstore	*Western Suburbs*
Field Museum of History--Shop	*Chicago Central*
Grand Tour World Travel Bookstore	*Chicago North*
J.T. Monckton Ltd.	*North*
Little Professor Book Center	*Western Suburbs*
The Little Book Shop Inc.	*Western Suburbs*
National Louis University Bookstore	*Northern Suburbs*
Plain Tales Books	*Northwest Suburbs*
Sandmeyer's Bookstore in Printer's Row	*Chicago Central*
The Savvy Traveller	*Chicago Central*

Women's Studies

Barbara's Bookstore	*Chicago North and Central*
Barbara's Bookstore	*Western Suburbs*
The Book Inn	*Southern Suburbs*
C.G. Jung Institute Bookstore	*Northern Suburbs*
Cokesbury	*Northwest Suburbs*
Left Bank Bookstall	*Western Suburbs*
Little Professor Book Center	*Western Suburbs*
National Louis University Bookstore	*Northern Suburbs*
Platypus Bookshop	*Northern Suburbs*
Stern's Book Service	*Chicago North*
Town House Books	*Western Suburbs*
Unabridged Books Inc.	*Chicago North*
UIC--Epi Center Bookstore	*Chicago West*
Women & Children First, Inc.	*Chicago North*

Zoology

Chicago Zoological Park Bookstore	*Western Suburbs*
Field Museum of History--Shop	*Chicago Central*
John G. Shedd Aquarium Sea Shop	*Chicago Central*
N. Fagin Books	*Northwest Suburbs*
W. Graham Arader III	*Chicago Central*

Alphabetical Index of Stores

Alphabetical Index of Stores

Alphabetical Index of Stores

Alphabetical Index of Stores

Reader Response Form

Please help us improve the next edition of *The Book Lover's Guide to Chicagoland*. If you've found any mistakes, if we've left anything out, or if a store's circumstances have changed, let us know! Any comments you have will be read and incorporated into the next edition. Send your comments to Lane Phalen, c/o Brigadoon Bay Books, P.O. Box 957724, Hoffman Estates, IL 60195.

Comments: _____
_____
_____
_____
_____
_____
_____

Your name and address: _____
_____
_____
_____

If you'd like to buy more copies of *The Book Lover's Guide to Chicagoland* and you can't find it at your local book store, you can order the book by mailing a copy of this form with a check or money order and sending them to:

Brigadoon Bay Books
Dept. C1
P.O. Box 957724
Hoffman Estates, IL 60195-7724

		Qty	
The Book Lover's Guide	($14.95 per book)	___	$_____
Shipping & Handling	($1.00 per book)		$_____
7.5% Sales Tax	($1.12 per book)		$_____
(Illinois addresses only)			
		Total	$_____

30 day money back guarantee!

Ship to:

_____
_____
_____
_____